Whatever Happened to the Gospel of Grace?

WHATEVER HAPPENED TO THE GOSPEL OF GRACE?

RECOVERING THE DOCTRINES THAT SHOOK THE WORLD

James Montgomery Boice

Foreword by Eric J. Alexander

CROSSWAY BOOKS • WHEATON, ILLINOIS
A DIVISION OF GOOD NEWS PUBLISHERS

Library of Congress Cataloging-in-Publication Data
Boice, James Montgomery, 1938-2000
   Whatever happened to the gospel of grace? : recovering the doctrines that shook the world / James Montgomery Boice ; foreword by Eric J. Alexander.
      p.   cm.
   Includes bibliographical references and index.
   ISBN 1-58134-237-3
   1. Grace (Theology)   I. Title.
BT761.2.B655   2001
230'.04624—dc21   00-012245
                                              CIP

15	14	13	12	11	10	09	08	07	06	05	04	03	02	01
15	14	13	12	11	10	9	8	7	6	5	4	3	2	1

To HIM

who loves us and has freed us

from our sins by his blood,

and has made us to be

a kingdom and priests

to serve his God and Father—

to him be glory and power

for ever and ever! Amen.

Revelation 1:5-6

Contents

Publisher's Foreword

꧁

This is an extraordinary kind of book. It is in fact the last written message of an extraordinary, perceptive, and godly man, Dr. James Montgomery Boice. As such it has a timeliness and urgency that the evangelical church today so critically needs to hear and heed. Stated simply as his last word, Jim Boice has given us a three-fold message, calling us as Christians: 1) to repent of our worldliness; 2) to recover the great salvation doctrines of the Bible as the Reformers did five hundred years ago; and 3) to live a life transformed by the essential truths of the gospel.

The urgency of our situation is seen especially in the first section of the book, where Dr. Boice shows how deeply evangelical Christians have been compromised by a thoroughgoing worldliness. In a manner remarkably parallel to the liberal church a generation ago, evangelicals today have embraced *the world's wisdom, the world's theology, the world's agenda, and the world's methods.* The result is an evangelical church that has lost the power and the reality of the gospel.

Though it is essential that we understand the urgency of our situation, the heart of Dr. Boice's message is a call to the recovery of the gospel (as found especially in the "doctrines that shook the world" five centuries ago) and a call to live out the gospel in every area of life. Thus Dr. Boice asks, "Can we have that power again in our day? We can. But only if we hold to the full-orbed Reformation gospel and do not compromise with the culture around us. . . . How does it happen? It happens by the renewing of our minds, . . . by study of the life-giving and renewing Word of God . . . empowered by the Holy Spirit [so that] we will begin to take on something of the glorious luster of the Lord Jesus Christ and will become increasingly like him."

We would do well then to hear and to heed this last message from Dr. Boice—a prophetic word to us, but equally a message of confident hope in the power of the gospel. As Dr. Boice wrote in the closing words of the book, "There are times in history when it takes a thousand voices to be heard as one voice. But there are other times, like our own, when one voice can ring forth as a thousand. So let's get on with our calling, and let those who say they know God show they actually do—for his glory and for the good of all."

Lane T. Dennis, President
Crossway Books

Foreword

꧀

At one o'clock on Friday, June 23, 2000, a vast company of people filled Tenth Presbyterian Church in Philadelphia. They had come from all over the world to honor the memory of Dr. James Montgomery Boice, pastor of the church for more than thirty years. The keynote of the service was heartfelt thanksgiving to God for such a remarkably fruitful life and ministry.

Eight weeks previously, the church was also crowded—for the opening service of the Philadelphia Conference on Reformation Theology (PCRT). During that conference, Dr. Boice shared with me the medical report he had received on Good Friday: He was suffering from cancer of the liver and the prognosis was very bad. He was planning to tell the congregation the following Sunday. This he did, with astonishing calmness, courage, and selflessness. Many said it was the most moving occasion they had ever shared in.

From his earliest days, Jim Boice was a leader among men. He distinguished himself at Harvard University, Princeton Seminary, and the University of Basel in Switzerland. His academic ability and scholarly nature were to become the foundation for a life dedicated to preaching, teaching, and defending the gospel.

His passion for reformed theology led him to found the PCRT in 1974. Similarly his concern for the Reformation principle of "sola Scriptura" lay behind his crucial influence in planning and convening the International Council on Biblical Inerrancy, from 1978 to 1988. In 1996 he was instrumental in forming the Alliance of Confessing Evangelicals.

Yet I do not think he would wish to be remembered mainly for these landmark conferences and their widespread influence. More than once he said to seminary students, to whom he frequently spoke, "I am first and foremost the pastor of Tenth Presbyterian Church. That's where my heart is."

Consistent with this, he spent more than thirty years as Tenth's senior minister, to its eternal benefit. Early in his ministry he wrote of the Puritans, "They were steeped in the Word of God. They were diligent. No work was too great or mountain too high for them to tackle. They were pious men who spent long hours in study and on their knees. They were not looking for promotion to positions of greater and greater prominence. Rather, they were willing to stay in one place, so the work of bringing the Word fully to that place might be completed." [1]

Theologically and personally, James Boice was himself in that true Puritan tradition. No man I have known has more fully than he exhibited and expounded in his life and ministry the five "solas" of which he writes in this book. They were the foundation stones of his thinking and the substance of his preaching.

Writing in these pages of the sufficiency of Christ for the believer, he says, "We need no other prophets to reveal God's word or will. We need no other priests to mediate God's salvation and blessing. We need no other kings to control the thinking and lives of believers. Jesus is everything to us and for us in the gospel."

So it was in Jim Boice's life. The more you got to know him, the more apparent that became. Quite simply, he lived to know Christ better; he lived to preach Christ more effectively; and he lived to exalt Christ with every faculty of his being.

His death brings great gain to him but great loss to the Christian church. Many of us miss him acutely, but we thank God that through such books as the one you now hold in your hand, and by many other means, "he, being dead, yet speaks."

Soli Deo gloria.

Eric J. Alexander
St. Andrews, Scotland

Preface

❖

Do we still believe in the gospel of grace? Consider Os Guinness's perceptive observation of contemporary church life. In a recent book he offers several telling examples of how some evangelicals have come to trust technology rather than the gospel and the power of God for winning the lost and achieving church growth. A Florida pastor with a 7,000-member church observed, "I must be doing right or things wouldn't be going so well." A Christian advertising agent, who has represented Coca-Cola as well as having developed the "I Found It" evangelistic campaign, expressed his "faith" in even more shocking terms:

> Back in Jerusalem where the church started, God performed a miracle there on the day of Pentecost. They didn't have the benefits of buttons and media, so God had to do a little supernatural work there. But today, with our technology, we have available to us the opportunity to create the same kind of interest in a secular society.

Another church growth consultant claims that "five to ten million baby boomers would be back in the fold within a month" if churches would only adopt three simple changes: 1) "Advertise," 2) Let people know about "product benefits," and 3) Be "nice to people."[1]

Has it come to that?

Apparently it has for some people, while others who would not express their trust in secular tools to accomplish spiritual work so brazenly nevertheless flirt with the world and its methods because the old ways no longer seem adequate to "get the job done." Really? Doesn't the gospel work anymore? Is the power of God really impotent in dealing with the particular challenges of our modern and postmodern age?

The leaders who have banded together as the Alliance of Confessing Evangelicals believe that the problem is not our failure to use secular tools but ignorance of God and neglect of the gospel of salvation through the work of the Lord Jesus Christ alone. We have achieved success—in a worldly sort of way. We have large churches with large budgets. We have immense commercial enterprises. But overall, church attendance in America has declined markedly in recent years (from a weekly high of about forty-six percent of the population to less than thirty-six percent today), and allegedly "born-again" people do not differ statistically in their beliefs and practices from their unbelieving neighbors. "We are living in a fool's paradise," said David Wells to a gathering of the National Association of Evangelicals several years ago.

The Alliance would like the evangelical church to recover its rich spiritual heritage by repenting of its rampant worldliness and by rediscovering the gospel of grace that meant so much to the Protestant Reformers. The Alliance purpose statement reads:

> The Alliance of Confessing Evangelicals exists to call the church, amidst our dying culture, to repent of its worldliness, to recover and confess the truth of God's Word as did the Reformers, and to see that truth embodied in doctrine, worship and life.[2]

This book follows the outline of the Alliance purpose statement, unfolding in three parts: 1) Our Dying Culture, 2) Doctrines That Shook the World, and 3) The Shape of Renewal. The heart of the book is part 2, in which the five great Reformation "*solas*" are explained: *sola Scriptura* ("Scripture alone"), *solus Christus* ("Christ alone"), *sola gratia* ("grace alone"), *sola fide* ("faith alone"), and *soli Deo gloria* ("glory to God alone").

This book is an expansion of a smaller booklet written for the Alliance, *What Makes a Church Evangelical?*[3] Those who have read that booklet will find some of its content here. Material has also been drawn from a few of my other writings, particularly the mate-

rial on the world and its ways of thinking in chapter 2. That chapter has been adapted, though with substantial changes, from parts
of *Mind Renewal in a Mindless Age: Preparing to Think and Act
Biblically.*[4]

Some readers may be interested in the poetry that is printed at
the start of each of these nine chapters. The lines are from new
hymns (words and music) written for the worship services of
Tenth Presbyterian Church in Philadelphia,[5] which I have served
as senior minister for more than thirty years. Instead of merely
complaining about the sad lack of biblical and doctrinal content in
most contemporary Christian music, we decided to do something
positive by producing new hymns. They are based on Bible texts
and focus on the doctrines unfolded in these pages.

We need a modern reformation—to recover the gospel of grace.
May God Almighty be pleased to grant it. For his glory alone.
Amen.

James Montgomery Boice
Philadelphia

Part One

OUR
DYING
CULTURE

ONE

❦

The New Pragmatism

'Round the throne in radiant glory
All creation loudly sings
Praise to God, to God Almighty—
Day and night the anthem rings:
"Holy, holy, holy, holy
Is our God, the King of kings."

These are not good days for the evangelical church, and anyone who takes a moment to evaluate the life and outlook of evangelical churches will understand that.

In recent years a number of books have been published in an effort to understand what is happening, and they are saying much the same thing even though their authors come from different backgrounds and are doing different work. I was struck by three studies that appeared within a year or two of each other. The first was *No Place for Truth*, by David F. Wells,[1] professor of historical and systematic theology at Gordon-Conwell Theological Seminary in Massachusetts. The second was *Power Religion*, by Michael Scott Horton,[2] vice president of the Alliance of Confessing Evangelicals. The third volume was *Ashamed of the Gospel*, by John MacArthur,[3] pastor of Grace Community Church in Sun Valley, California. Each of these authors was writing about the evangelical church, and one can get an idea of what each is saying just from the titles alone.

Yet the subtitles are even more revealing. The subtitle of Wells's book is *Or Whatever Happened to Evangelical Theology?* The subtitle of Horton's book is *The Selling Out of the Evangelical Church.* The subtitle of MacArthur's work proclaims *When the Church Becomes Like the World.*

When we put them together we realize that these careful observers of the current scene perceive that evangelicalism is seriously off-base today because it has abandoned its evangelical truth-heritage. The thesis of Wells's book is that the evangelical church is either dead or dying as a significant religious force because it has forgotten what it stands for. Instead of trying to do God's work in God's way, it is trying to build a prosperous earthly kingdom with secular tools. Thus, as we have noted, Wells declared that, in spite of our apparent success, we have been "living in a fool's paradise."

John H. Armstrong, founder and president of Reformation and Revival Ministries, edited a volume titled *The Coming Evangelical Crisis.*[4] When I asked him whether he thought the crisis was still coming or is actually here, he admitted that in his judgment the crisis is already upon us.

"And why is that?" I continued.

He answered, "It is because evangelicals have forgotten their theology."

A THIRTY-YEAR PERSPECTIVE

Let me put my thoughts in historical perspective. When I returned to the United States from theological studies in Europe in 1966 to work at *Christianity Today,* I found that the 1960s were a time of rising influence for evangelicals. *Christianity Today* was part of the resurgence. Under the leadership of founding editor Carl F. H. Henry, the magazine was mounting an effective challenge to the liberal churches and especially to the liberal theological journal *The Christian Century.* The largest seminaries in the country were evangelical, some with thousands of students. Evangelical churches also were growing, and they were emerging from their comfortable suburban ghettos to engage selected aspects of the secular culture.

Observing this trend exactly a decade later, *Newsweek* magazine would call 1976 "the year of the evangelical."

It was also a time of decline for the mainline churches. I was part of one of those denominations from 1968 to 1980, and I came to the conclusion that the mainline churches were trying to do God's work in a secular way and that they were declining as a result. The older churches were pursuing the world's wisdom, embracing the world's theology, following the world's agenda, and employing the world's methods.

1. *The world's wisdom.* In earlier ages of the church, Christians stood before their Bibles and confessed their ignorance of spiritual things. They even confessed their inability to understand what was written in the Bible except for the grace of God through the ministry of the Holy Spirit to unfold the Bible's wisdom to them. They sought the wisdom of God in Scripture. But this ancient wisdom had been set aside by the liberal church, with the result that the reforming voice of God in the church through the Scriptures was forgotten. The liberal denominations had been undermined by rationalism, and they were no longer able to receive the Bible as God's Word to man, only as man's word about God. The Bible might still be true overall or in places, they believed, but it could no longer be regarded as authoritative.

This had three sad consequences for these churches. First, it produced a state of uncertainty about what to believe. This was usually disguised, often by increasingly elaborate liturgies or by social programs. But it was the true case, and it explained why so many people were beginning to desert these churches and turn to conservative churches instead. Unable to redirect the bureaucracies by personal participation or by democratic vote, people began voting with their feet and either dropped out entirely or turned to those churches that still retained a biblical message.

About this time a churchman named Dean Kelley wrote a book titled *Why Conservative Churches Are Growing*.[5] He said it was because they knew what they believed. He was right. People are not attracted to churches that do not know where they stand theologically.

Second, the liberal churches were embracing the outlook and moral values of the world. Since there was nothing to make them distinct, they ended up being merely a pale reflection of the culture in which they were functioning.

Third, they made decisions based not on the teachings of the Bible but as a response to the prevailing opinions of the time, what Francis Schaeffer called the wisdom of the fifty-one percent vote. Business was done by consensus. Issues would be discussed (usually with very little reference to the Bible or its principles), a vote would be taken, a majority carried the day, and the moderator would usually declare, "The Holy Spirit has spoken." For the most part, I thought that the Holy Spirit had very little to do with what happened. But I also learned that if Christians throw out a transcendent authority, another authority will always come in to take the Bible's place.

2. *The world's theology.* The mainline churches had also adopted the world's theology. The world's theology is easy to define. It is the view that human beings are basically good, that no one is really lost, and that belief in Jesus Christ is not necessary for anyone's salvation—though it may be helpful for some people. In popular terms it is the "I'm OK, you're OK" philosophy.

In adopting this theology the liberal churches did not entirely abandon the traditional biblical terminology, of course. They could hardly have done that and still have pretended to be Christian. Many of the old biblical terms were retained, but they were given different meanings. *Sin* became not rebellion against God and his righteous law, for which we are held accountable, but ignorance or the oppression found in social structures. It was what the young people were shouting about in the 1960s. The way to overcome was by social change, new laws, or revolution. *Jesus* became not the incarnate God who died for our salvation but rather a pattern for creative living. We were to look to Jesus as an example, but not as a divine Savior. Some looked to him as a model revolutionary. *Salvation* was defined as liberation from oppressive social structures. *Faith* was becoming aware of oppression and beginning to do something about it. *Evangelism* did not mean carrying the gospel of Jesus Christ to a perishing world but rather working through or against the world's power centers to overthrow entrenched injustice.

3. *The world's agenda.* In the liberal churches the words "the world must set the agenda" were quite popular. That had been the theme of the 1964 gathering of the World Council of Churches, and it meant that the church's concerns should be the concerns of the world, even to the exclusion of the gospel. If the world's main priority was world hunger, that should be the church's priority too. Racism? Ecology? Aging? Whatever it was, it was to be first in the concerns of Christian people.

4. *The world's methods.* The final accommodation of the mainline churches to the world was in the realm of methods. The methods God has given for us to do his work are participation, persuasion, and prayer. But these three methods, particularly persuasion and prayer, were being jettisoned by the mainline churches as hopelessly inadequate, and what was proposed in their place was a gospel of power politics and money. I saw a cartoon in *The New Yorker* at about that time that I thought got it exactly right. Two Pilgrims were coming over on the Mayflower and one was saying to the other, "Religious freedom is my immediate goal, but my long-range plan is to go into real estate."

I was reminded of that cartoon years later when I heard the Reverend Phillip Jensen, the evangelical senior minister of St. Mathias Anglican Church in Sydney, Australia, say that in his opinion the major denominations are nothing more than real estate holding companies.

THE WORLDLY (EVANGELICAL) CHURCHES

But here is the important thing. What has hit me like a thunderbolt in recent years is the discovery that what I had been saying about the liberal churches at the end of the 1960s and in the '70s now needs to be said about evangelical churches too.

Can it be that evangelicals, who have always opposed liberalism and its methods, have now also fixed their eyes on a worldly kingdom and have made politics and money their weapons of choice for winning it? I think they have. About ten years ago Martin Marty, always a shrewd observer of the American church, said in a magazine interview that, in his judgment, by the end of the century evangelicals would be "the most worldly people in America." He was exactly on target when he said that, except that he was probably a bit too cautious. Evangelicals fulfilled his prophecy before the turn of the millennium.

1. *The world's wisdom.* Evangelicals are not heretics, at least not consciously. If we ask whether the Bible is the authoritative and inerrant Word of God, most will answer affirmatively, at least if the question is asked in traditional ways. Is the Bible God's Word? Of course! All evangelicals know that. Is it authoritative? Yes, that too. Inerrant? Most evangelicals will affirm inerrancy. But many evangelicals have abandoned the Bible all the same simply because they do not think it is adequate for the challenges we face today. They do not think it is sufficient for winning people to Christ in this age, so they turn to felt-need sermons or entertainment or "signs and wonders" instead. They do not think the Bible is sufficient for achieving Christian growth, so they turn to therapy groups or Christian counseling. They do not think it is sufficient for making God's will known, so they look for external signs or revelations. They do not think it is adequate for changing our society, so they establish evangelical lobby groups in Washington and work to elect "Christian" congressmen, senators, presidents, and other officials. They seek change by power politics and money.

2. *The world's theology.* Like the liberals before us, evangelicals use the Bible's words but give them new meaning, pouring bad secular content into spiritual terminology. But differently, of course. We live in a therapeutic age now. So evangelicals have recast their theology in psychiatric terms. *Sin* has become dysfunctional behavior. *Salvation* is self-esteem or wholeness. *Jesus* is more of an example for right living than our Savior from sin and God's wrath. Sunday by Sunday people are told how to have happy marriages and raise nice children, but not how to get right with God.

The problem here is that sin is not dysfunction, though it may contribute to it. "Sin is any want of conformity unto, or transgression of, the law of God" (Westminster Shorter Catechism, Answer to Question 14), and our major problem is not a lack of wholeness or a lack of integration of personalities but the peril of God's wrath toward us for our sin. What we need from God in Christ is not an example for living but an atonement. Even preaching about happy marriages and raising nice children is wrong if it leads people to suppose that, if they succeed in these areas, everything is well with them whether or not they have repented of their sin, trusted Jesus Christ as their Savior, and are following him as their Lord.

3. *The world's agenda.* The world's major agenda—forget world hunger, racism, or ecology—is to be happy—happiness being understood, as Francis Schaeffer put it in several of his books, as the maximum amount of personal peace and sufficient affluence to enjoy it. But is that not the bottom line of much evangelical preaching today? To be happy? To be contented? To be satisfied? Some of the worst forms of this particularly Western form of worldliness are seen in the health, wealth, and prosperity preachers, who claim that it is God's desire that his people be rich and feel satisfied. But it is also seen in preaching that extols the good life as a valid Christian goal while failing to address the sins of those who are living for themselves rather than for others. Far be it from many Christians today to preach a gospel that would expose sin and drive men and women to the Savior—or demand a hard following after Jesus Christ as the only true discipleship.

4. *The world's methods.* Evangelicals have become like liberals in this area too. How else are we to explain the emphasis so many place on numerical growth, large physical plants, and money? Or so many bizarre approaches to evangelism? Or that so many pastors tone down the hard edges of biblical truth in order to attract greater numbers to their services? Or that we major in entertainment? Or that so many support a National Association of

Evangelicals lobby in Washington? Or that we have created social action groups to advance specific legislation?

Not long ago I came across a newspaper story about a church that is trying to attract worshipers by imitating radio news programs that promise: "Give us twenty-two minutes, and we'll give you the world." Their 9:00 A.M. Sunday service is called "Express Worship," and the hook is that parishioners can come in and be out in twenty-two minutes. In one service described by the newspaper, the pastor began with a greeting and a short prayer, followed by a reading from Luke 7:1-10. He then asked the worshipers to write down their thoughts on what constitutes authority in their lives. Finally, they sang "What a Friend We Have in Jesus" and went out. The pastor described it as "a restructuring of the way we think of the service. Not one person delivering the truth to you, but a shared experience."

The newspaper said, "Give him twenty-two minutes, and he'll give you the Lord."

Here is another example. An evangelical church in Philadelphia recently distributed a brochure giving "ten reasons" to visit their Sunday evening service:

1. The air conditioning feels great.
2. Coffee and goodies for everyone after every service.
3. The music is upbeat and easy to sing.
4. You get to meet some really neat people.
5. The sermon is always relevant to everyday life.
6. You can sleep in on Sundays and still make it to church on time.
7. Child care and children's church are provided.
8. Free parking!
9. You can go to the shore for the weekend and still make it to church on Sunday night.
10. You will discover an awesome God who cares about you.

When I saw that I was reminded of an advertising brochure I had come across some years before. See if you can guess what is being described. This brochure was printed in full color with pictures of attractive people, and the cover read: "This Is Where It's At." Inside it had headings like these:

It's about family.
It's about style.
It's about giving.
It's about fun.
It's about the best way to please everybody.
It's about caring.

Actually, the brochure was an advertisement for the Liberty Tree Mall in Danvers, Massachusetts. But its appeal is virtually undistinguishable from that of the churches I am describing.

Or, to follow a different line, consider evangelical rhetoric. Evangelicals speak of "taking back America," "fighting for the country's soul," "reclaiming the United States for Christ." How? By electing Christian presidents, congressmen, and senators, lobbying for conservative judges, taking over power structures, and imposing our Christian standard of morality on the rest of the nation by law. But we ought to ask: Was America ever really a Christian nation? Was any nation ever really Christian? Does law produce morality? What about Augustine's doctrine of the two cities—the city of man and the city of God—which meant so much to the Reformers? Will any country ever be anything other than man's city? And what about America's soul? Is there really an American soul to be redeemed or fought over?

Recently a book appeared written by two people who had been active in the Moral Majority movement in the first half of the 1980s. It is titled *Blinded by Might*, and its authors are Cal Thomas, now a syndicated religion columnist appearing in more than 475 newspapers nationwide, and Ed Dobson, pastor of Calvary Church in Grand Rapids, Michigan. Thomas and Dobson saw the years 1980–1985 as a period of tremendous opportunity for Christians, and they believe there were significant achievements. The Moral Majority focused public discussion on moral issues. It drew attention to the role of religion and religious people in the political process. It awakened millions of formerly dormant Christians to their civic responsibility. Still, Thomas and Dobson judge the movement to have been a failure, because they believe they were trying to achieve the renewal of the country through a political process, which does not and cannot happen, rather than from the bottom up through lives that have been changed by God. "We failed because we were unable to redirect a nation from the top down," they concluded. "Real change must come from the bottom up or, better yet, from the inside out."[6]

And failure was not the only problem. Along the way evangelicals were seduced by the allure of worldly power. Quoting 2 Corinthians 10:3-6, which says that the Christian's true weapons are not the weapons of this world but the weapons of truth, persuasion, and character, the authors write, "The strongholds and pretensions [of this world] can only be demolished under two conditions: one, that we don't fight with the world's weapons, but with divine ones; and two, that our obedience is complete. We have been trying to use the world's weapons of political power, and we have not been sufficiently obedient to the call of Jesus to care as he cares and do as he did."[7] Their summary:

> We don't have a shortage of leaders, but a shortage of followers of the one Leader who can transform lives and nations. We don't need to enlarge our vision, but make it smaller and more focused. We don't need more numbers, but more quality and consistency among the numbers we already have. We need more people who will do things God's way and fewer people doing things man's way.[8]

These are strong words. But they come from people who have walked the path of political power and have found it to lead nowhere.

When you put these contemporary evangelical characteristics together—pursuit of the world's wisdom, acceptance of the world's theology, adoption of the world's agenda, and utilization of the world's methods—it is hard to escape the feeling that today's evangelicals have fallen into the trap of the liberals before them. Much of the time they sound like the liberal journal *The Christian Century* that *Christianity Today* was founded to oppose. And as for *Christianity Today* itself, it has become a lot like *The Christian Century* was, though with far less theological content.

THE ONSLAUGHT OF THE MODERN

A major part of the problem is the onslaught of the modern age. The dominant philosophy of today's generation is relativism, the rejection of absolutes (as described by Allan Bloom in his best-selling book on higher education, *The Closing of the American Mind*[9]), and the substitution of pragmatism for truth. Moreover, hard on the heels of philosophical relativism came the militant attack on beliefs or values of any kind known popularly as postmodernity.

Evangelicals seem to have succumbed to this spirit.

If truth is relative, as the majority of people living in our age believe, then one idea is as good as another, and the only criteria for choosing one course of action rather than another are: 1) pragmatism (does it accomplish what we want?) and 2) pleasure (do we feel good after we have done it?). Instead of people saying that they agree or disagree with a statement, they respond that they either "like" or "dislike" it. We no longer ask people, "What do you think about this?" We ask them, "How do you feel about it?" Few are guided by principle any longer, only by what they prefer. "You have to decide what's right for you," we are told. In such a climate, the only remaining virtue is tolerance, and the only philosophies that are wrong are those that believe in truth.

Evangelicals deny that they also think this way, but the facts undermine their denials. Recent polls by sociologists such as George Gallup, Jr., and George Barna show that the majority of evangelicals no longer believe in absolute truth. Seventy-six percent believe that human beings are, by nature, basically good. Eighty-six percent believe that, in salvation, "God helps those who help themselves." Evangelicals used to be defined by their theology. But today they are increasingly defined by their style. They used to seek pastors who knew the Bible. Today they search for ministers with entertainment and management skills. They flock to dynamic pulpit personalities rather than to those who exhibit godly character.

In a recent article Gene E. Veith describes the impact of our postmodern times on two things: 1) the content of preaching and 2) the church growth movement:

> In a "mega-shift" away from classic Protestant theology, many evangelicals are proclaiming a touchy-feely, therapeutic god who is light years away from the Holy One of Israel. This is a god of tolerance, who condemns no one and who can be reached by many different paths. Instead of the forgiveness of sins, the mega-shift preachers offer the gospel of a good self-image and earthly success through positive thinking.
>
> Often accompanying mega-shift theology is the church growth movement, which seeks to build mega-churches by adjusting Christianity to the desires of the culture. Doctrine does not go over well in an age of relativism, so in order to attract new members, theological content must be minimized. Nor do people wish to hear about sin, so the church must cultivate an atmosphere of moral tolerance. Since people choose their religious beliefs not so much on the basis of whether they are true but whether they "like" the particular church, the life of the congregation must be made as pleasant and undemanding as possible. The exaltation of the pleasure-principle means that worship services above all must be entertaining. The exaltation of the will means that the customers must be given what they want.[10]

Some of these changes are unconscious, of course. But they are nonetheless serious and may eventually be fatal for those who have embraced them uncritically. How can we who are evangelicals decry the world when we are seemingly so hell-bent on imitating it? How can we denounce humanism when we are so blatantly man-centered ourselves?

The central reality for evangelicals, as for all others who name the name of Christ, is that Christianity is a religion of truth. It is based on certain facts of history that concern the revelation of God to his people and his salvation of those people by the work of his

Son. Wherever that is forgotten or lost, as it is being lost in our day, Christianity ceases to remain truly Christian and becomes only another religiously oriented self-help program. Veith says rightly that Christianity thrives "not by trying to offer people what they already have, but by offering them what they desperately lack— namely, the Word of God and salvation through Jesus Christ."[11]

THE ALLIANCE OF CONFESSING EVANGELICALS

Is the situation hopeless? Is there really any hope that the church will return to the gospel of grace? Some would say so. But nothing can ever be hopeless where God and his gospel are concerned. The Alliance of Confessing Evangelicals is one organization that has been formed to address the situation. It began in 1994 when a group of leaders met to discuss the decline they were seeing in evangelicalism and to ask whether something might be done to revive the evangelical churches. After an informal meeting in Philadelphia in February of that year, a larger group of fifteen leaders met in September for a strategic planning conference in Orlando, Florida, where discussion of common concerns gave birth to this new effort. As noted in the preface to this book, the Alliance adopted the following mission statement:

> The Alliance of Confessing Evangelicals exists to call the church, amidst our dying culture, to repent of its worldliness, to recover and confess the truth of God's Word as did the Reformers, and to see that truth embodied in doctrine, worship and life.

The next step was to gather one hundred and twenty evangelical pastors, teachers, and leaders of parachurch organizations in Cambridge, Massachusetts (April 1996) to produce the "Cambridge Declaration."[12] This declaration was the product of four days of meetings in which papers were presented on four subjects: "Our Dying Culture," "The Truths of God's Word," "Repentance, Recovery and Confession," and "The Reformation of the Church in Doctrine, Worship and Life." The declaration, which flowed from the papers, argued that chief among the truths evangelicals need to recover are the great Reformation doctrines summarized by the well-known *solas* (Latin for "only" or "alone"): *sola Scriptura*, which means "Scripture alone"; *solus Christus*, which means "Christ alone"; *sola gratia*, which means "grace alone"; *sola fide*, which means "faith alone"; and *soli Deo gloria*, which means "glory to God alone."

Some matters of theology and church government are debatable and will undoubtedly be so until Jesus comes again. This will be true even among the most biblical theologians and the most sincere believers. Moreover, most leaders recognize that not everything that is desirable for the church, including these debatable matters, however important some of them may be, is essential for the church's survival. But these qualifications do not apply here. Without these five confessional statements—Scripture alone, Christ alone, grace alone, faith alone, and glory to God alone—we do not have a true church, and certainly not one that will survive for very long. For how can any church be a true and faithful church if it does not stand for Scripture alone, is not committed to a biblical gospel, and does not exist for God's glory? A church without these convictions has ceased to be a true church, whatever else it may be.

1. *Scripture alone*. When the Reformers used the words *sola Scriptura* ("Scripture alone") they were expressing their concern for the Bible's authority, and what they meant to say by those words is that the Bible alone is our ultimate authority—not the pope, not the church, not the traditions of the church or church councils, still less personal intimations or subjective feelings, but Scripture only. Other sources of authority may have an important role to play. Some are even established by God—such as the authority of church elders, the authority of the state, or the authority of parents over children. But Scripture alone is truly ultimate. Therefore, if any of these other authorities depart from Bible teaching, they are to be judged by the Bible and rejected.

Sola Scriptura has been called the formal principle of the

Reformation, meaning that it stands at the very beginning and thus gives form or direction to all that Christians affirm as Christians. Evangelicals abandon *sola Scriptura* when they reinterpret the Bible to fit modern notions of reality or ignore it on the basis of supposed private divine revelations or leadings.

At the beginning of 1978, I became chairman of the International Council on Biblical Inerrancy, an organization that made an important contribution to evangelical thought. The inerrancy of the Bible is a critical doctrine. We were right to defend it and had some important successes in doing so. However, important as that matter was, I do not think the inerrancy of the Bible is the most important Scripture issue facing the church as we move into the early years of the third millennium. The issue I would pinpoint today is the *sufficiency* of God's Word, meaning: Do we really believe that in this book God has given us what we need to do all necessary spiritual work? Or do we think we have to supplement the Bible with man-made techniques or devices? Consider these questions about four important areas of the church's work:

Evangelism: Do we need sociological techniques to do evangelism? Must we attract people to our churches by showmanship and entertainment?

Sanctification: Do we need psychology and psychiatry for Christian growth? Are encounter groups essential?

Discerning God's will: Do we need extra-biblical signs or miracles for guidance? Does God speak by personal revelations or "in our hearts"?

Impacting society: Is the Bible's teaching adequate for achieving social progress and reform?

Unfortunately, it is possible to believe that the Bible is the inerrant Word of God, the only infallible rule of faith and practice, as many if not all evangelicals claim to do, and still effectually to repudiate it because we think that it does not work today and are convinced that other things need to be brought in to accomplish what the Bible cannot do.

2. *Christ alone.* The church of the Middle Ages spoke about Christ. A church that failed to do that could hardly claim to be Christian. But the medieval church had added many human achievements to Christ's work, so that it was no longer possible to say that salvation was entirely by Christ and his atonement. Christ was part of it, even the major part. But salvation was also said to be won by human merit, especially the merit of the saints. The saints were said to have been so exceptionally holy that they had accumulated masses of excess merit that could be applied to lesser believers by the sacraments through church authority. The church was able to effect salvation by tapping into this "treasury of merit." This was the most basic of all heresies, as the Reformers rightly perceived. It was the work of God *plus* the work of man, Jesus' righteousness *plus* our own righteousness.

The Reformation motto *solus Christus* ("Christ alone") was formed to repudiate this error. It affirmed that salvation has been accomplished once for all by the mediatorial work of the historical Jesus Christ alone. His sinless life and substitutionary atonement alone are sufficient for our justification, and any "gospel" that fails to acknowledge that or denies it is a false gospel that will save no one. Because the Roman Catholic Church was teaching this false gospel, the Reformers declared that it was a false or apostate church.

3. *Grace alone.* The words *sola gratia* ("grace alone") mean that human beings have no claim upon God. That is, God owes us nothing except just punishment for our many and very willful sins. Therefore, if he does save sinners, which he does in the case of some but not all, it is only because it pleases him to do it. Indeed, apart from this grace and the regenerating work of the Holy Spirit that flows from it, no one would be saved, since in our lost condition human beings are not capable of winning, seeking out, or even cooperating with God's grace. By insisting on "grace alone" the Reformers were denying that human methods, techniques, or strategies in themselves could ever bring anyone to faith. It is grace

alone expressed through the supernatural work of the Holy Spirit that brings us to Christ, releasing us from our bondage to sin and raising us from death to spiritual life.

4. *Faith alone.* The Reformers never tired of saying that "justification is by grace alone through faith alone because of Christ alone." When put into theological shorthand the doctrine was expressed as "justification by faith alone," the article by which the church stands or falls, according to Martin Luther. The Reformers called justification by faith Christianity's "material principle," because it involves the very matter or substance of what a person must understand and believe to be saved. Justification is a declaration of God based on the work of Christ. It flows from God's grace and it comes to the individual not by anything he or she might do but by "faith alone." We may state the full doctrine as:

> Justification is the act of God by which he declares sinners to be righteous because of Christ alone, by grace alone, through faith alone.

This is what Paul teaches in Romans 3:21-26, verses that include each of these elements. They refer to a righteousness that is not our own but is instead a righteousness from God revealed from heaven (v. 21). They speak of God's grace ("justified freely by his grace," v. 24). They talk about faith; the word appears eight times in verses 21-31. And this is said to be possible because of Christ alone: "This righteousness from God comes through faith in Jesus Christ" (v. 22), and we are "justified freely by his grace through the redemption that came by Christ Jesus" (v. 24).

5. *Glory to God alone.* Each of the great *solas*—"Scripture alone" (*sola Scriptura*), "Christ alone" (*solus Christus*), "grace alone" (*sola gratia*) and "faith alone" (*sola fide*)—is summed up in the fifth Reformation motto: *soli Deo gloria,* meaning "to God alone be the glory." It is what the apostle Paul expressed in Romans 11:36 when he wrote, "to him be the glory forever! Amen." These words follow naturally from the preceding words, "For from him and through him and to him are all things" (v. 36), since it is

because all things really are from God, through God, and to God, that we say "to God alone be the glory."

I will be arguing in this book that, although there are many reasons for the desertion of the Reformation gospel by today's evangelicals—among them obsession with the culture, a consumer mentality, and a recasting of the gospel in worldly terms to appeal to unbelievers—the chief problem is that we have forgotten God and are not really living for his glory. In the church of the Middle Ages, God's glory was acknowledged though diminished by ascribing so much false credit to man or to the church and its sacraments. The problem today is that we hardly think of God at all, and the reason we do not think about him is that we have forgotten the meaning and importance of these essential doctrines.

WHAT CAN I DO NOW?

Can anything be done about the current problems within evangelical churches? The Alliance of Confessing Evangelicals believes that something can be done, but it will not be easy. The opening statement of the Cambridge Declaration says, "Evangelical churches today are increasingly dominated by the spirit of this age rather than by the Spirit of Christ. As evangelicals, we call ourselves to repent of this sin and to recover the historic Christian faith." This calls for three things:

1. *We must recognize and understand the problem.* The problem is that we are "dominated by the spirit of this age," even though we appear to have right doctrines and believe the right things.

Several decades ago, when the conservative rebirth was getting underway, evangelical churches and organizations were held together by varieties of a typical "creed" or statement of faith. It usually had about twelve points, starting with God or the Bible; affirming the deity of Christ, his virgin birth, and resurrection; acknowledging the Great Commission; and concluding with statements about Christ's visible bodily return and the final judgment. These short evangelical creeds avoided most divisive matters. They did not refer to the church; they ignored the sacraments; they passed by the sovereignty of God in salvation and the inability of lost people to respond to the gospel apart from God's grace. Nevertheless, as far as they went, they stated their short list of non-negotiables with clarity.

In spite of their obvious weaknesses, especially when compared to the powerful creeds of the Reformation, these evangelical faith statements seemed to work well at holding evangelicals to a supernatural gospel. But it would seem also that evangelical strength actually lay in the fact that the Christians involved knew more of their Bibles and had deeper theological commitments than their truncated creeds suggested. Most were part of some ecclesiastical tradition going back to the Reformation; and many members of evangelical churches who were not actually Christians held to something like a Christian world- and life-view.

All of that has disappeared. Very few people have anything like a Christian world- and life-view today, and we are discovering that—in a secular and increasingly hostile culture—mild evangelical consensus statements are inadequate. For all its apparent strength, evangelicalism has become weak at the center, and the result has been the surrender to the world's wisdom, theology, agenda, and methods described earlier. Instead of reducing our affirmations in this way, we need to recover and proclaim the gospel of grace—a robust, full-orbed theology with a transcendent view of God and an informed focus on the doctrines of his grace.

2. *We must repent of this sin.* People do not like to talk about sin today, but sin is our problem and we must talk about it and deal with it if we are to move forward. When we talk about repenting of this sin we mean that our doctrinal failure is an offense against God and is therefore something for which we need seriously to repent. The very first of "The Ninety-five Theses" prepared by Martin Luther said, "When our Lord and Master, Jesus Christ, said 'repent,' he meant that the entire life of believers should be one of repentance." If that is true of "the entire life of believers," it is certainly true of our first and standing obligation to defend and proclaim the gospel, which we have failed to do.

3. *We must recover the historic Christian faith.* This will require

serious study of the Bible, and for some it will involve a radical reordering of their entire perspectives, not to mention the way they have been going about their Christian work. For all, it will mean a new reliance on the power of the Holy Spirit to work through the teaching and preaching of God's Word, rather than a frantic search for some tantalizing new methodology to persuade unbelievers to attend and join our churches.

In 1524, seven years after Martin Luther had nailed his Ninety-five Theses to the door of the Castle Church at Wittenberg, the farmers of Germany rebelled against their feudal lords in what became known as The Peasants' War (1524–1526). It began near Schaffhausen, where Hans Mueller, acting on a suggestion from Thomas Muenzer, formed the peasants into an "Evangelical Brotherhood" pledged to emancipate the farmers. By the end of that year there were 30,000 farmers in arms in southern Germany refusing to pay state taxes, church tithes, or feudal dues. In March 1525, they drafted and circulated widely a document called the "Twelve Articles," in which they claimed the right to choose their own pastors, pay only just tithes, be considered as free men rather than serfs, enjoy fair rents, and make other reasonable demands. They were also favorable to the Reformation and opposed to the Roman Catholic Church.

The peasants sent a copy of the articles to Luther, fully expecting his support. And, indeed, Luther's first response was sympathetic. He acknowledged the injustices about which the farmers were in arms and blamed the rulers of both state and church for their plight. But Luther did not endorse the rebellion, even though the majority of its goals coincided with those of the Reformation. And later, when hundreds of monasteries were sacked and many cities overrun, Luther denounced the violence in characteristically fierce terms. Why did Luther react this way, when nearly everyone, the peasants above all, expected him to side with them? Luther's justified fear of anarchy was one strong reason. Another was his belief that God had established the authority of princes. To rebel against the powers that exist is to rebel against God, he said.

Luther also knew that the power of the sword has not been

given either to the church or to the individual Christian, and he was aware that our weapons are not the weapons of this world. It is the power of God operating through the teaching of his Word that alone has power "to demolish strongholds" (2 Cor. 10:4). According to Luther, the Reformation would proceed *non vi, sed verbo*—not by force, but by the power of God's Word. And it did! The Peasants' War was a tragic episode in the Reformation period. As far as Germany was concerned, more lives were lost in that war than in any tumult prior to the Thirty Years' War, which came about a century later (1618–1648). Some 130,000 farmers died in battle or afterward as a result of harsh retaliation. The Reformation itself almost perished. But it did not, because it was moving forward by the power of the Word of God, as God blessed the teaching and influence of the Reformers.

Can we have that power again in our day? We can. But only if we hold to the full-orbed Reformation gospel and do not compromise with the culture around us, as we have been doing. If we hold to these doctrines, our churches and those we influence will grow stronger, while other churches go the way of the liberals before us, not vanishing entirely but becoming increasingly insignificant as an effective religious force.

The Pattern of This Age

Give praise to God who reigns above
For perfect knowledge, wisdom, love;
His judgments are divine, devout,
His paths beyond all tracing out.
Come, lift your voice to heaven's high throne,
And glory give to God alone!

Some Bible passages are enriched when we read them in other translations, and Romans 12:2 is one such passage: "Do not conform any longer to the pattern of this world." This sentence has two key words: "world," which is actually "age" (*aion*, meaning, "this present age" in contrast to "the age to come"); and "do not conform," which is a compound having at its root the word "scheme." So the verse means, "Do not let the age in which you live force you into its scheme of thinking and behaving." This is what some of the translations bring out. The Catholic New American Bible says, "Do not conform yourself to this age." The Jerusalem Bible says, "Do not model yourselves on the behavior of the world around you." *The Living Bible* reads, "Don't copy the behavior and customs of this world." Best known is the paraphrase of J. B. Phillips: "Don't let the world around you squeeze you into its own mold." The idea in each of these translations is that the world has its ways of thinking and doing things and is exerting pressure on Christians to conform to it. But instead of being conformed to the world, Christians are to be changed from within to be increasingly like Jesus Christ.

Romans 12:2 is a natural starting point to follow up on the concerns expressed in the last chapter. For if what we discovered in chapter 1 is right, the chief problem with the evangelical church is that we have been increasingly conformed to this world's patterns and that, if we are to see a new reformation, we will have to break away from these patterns and seek to recover the authentic biblical gospel, learning again to think and act in God's way.

The first phrase of Romans 12:2 is a warning against worldliness, of course. But as soon as we use the word *worldly* we have to make clear what real worldliness is. When I was growing up in a fundamentalist church I was taught that worldliness was such pursuits as smoking, drinking, dancing, and playing cards. A Christian girl might say, "I don't smoke, and I don't chew, and I don't go with boys who do." But that is not what Romans 12:2 is about. To think of worldliness only in those terms is to trivialize what is a far more serious and far more subtle problem.

The clue to what is in view here is that in the next phrase Paul urges, as an alternative to being "conformed" to this world, being "transformed *by the renewing of your mind.*" This means that he is concerned about a way of thinking rather than merely a way of behaving, though right behavior will follow naturally if our thinking is set straight. The worldliness we are to break away from and repudiate is the world's "worldview," what the Germans call *Weltanschauung,* a comprehensive, systematic way of looking at all things. We are to break out of the world's categories of thinking and allow our minds to be molded by the Word of God instead.

In our day Christians have not done this very well, and that is the reason why they are so often "worldly" in the other senses too. In fact, it is a sad commentary on our churches, verified by numerous polls, that Christians in general have nearly the same thoughts, values, and behavior patterns as the world around them.

SECULARISM: "THE COSMOS IS ALL THAT IS"

If worldliness is not smoking, drinking, dancing, and playing cards, what is it? If it is a way of thinking, what is a worldly "worldview"? This is something we need to approach in a variety of ways, since there is no single word that is perfectly descriptive of how the world thinks. Nevertheless, if there is any word that describes today's way of thinking more than others, it is *secularism*. Secularism is an umbrella term that covers a number of other "isms," such as humanism, relativism, materialism, and pragmatism. But secularism, more than any other single word, aptly describes the mental framework and value structure of the people of our time.

The word *secular* also comes closest to what Paul actually says when he refers to "the pattern of this world" in Romans 12. Secular is derived from the Latin word *saeculum,* which means "age," and the word Paul uses in verse 2 is the exact Greek equivalent. The New International Version uses the word "world," but the Greek actually says, "Do not be conformed to this age." In other words, "Do not be 'secular' in your worldview."

There is a right way to be secular, of course. Christians live in the world and are therefore rightly concerned about this world's affairs. We vote in elections and have other legitimate secular interests. But secularism (note the "ism") is more than this. It is a philosophy that does not see beyond the world but operates as if this age is all there is.

The best single statement of secularism I know is something Carl Sagan said in the television series *Cosmos.* He was pictured standing before a spectacular view of the heavens with its many swirling galaxies, saying in a hushed, almost reverential tone, "The cosmos is all that is or ever was or ever will be." That is "secularism in your face." It is a worldview bound up entirely by the limits of the material universe, by what we can see and touch and weigh and measure. If we think in terms of our existence here, it means operating within the limits of life on earth. If we are thinking of time, it means disregarding the eternal and thinking only of the "now."

Secularism is expressed in popular advertising slogans such as "You only go around once" and the "Now Generation." These slogans dominate our culture and express an outlook that has become increasingly harmful. If "now" is the only time that matters, why should we worry about the national debt, for example? Let our children worry about it. Or why should we study hard preparing to do meaningful work later on in life, as long as we can enjoy ourselves now? Most important, why should I worry about God or righteousness or sin or judgment or salvation, if there is no beyond and now is all that matters? R. C. Sproul says:

> For secularism, all life, every human value, every human activity must be understood in light of this present time. . . . What matters is *now* and only *now.* All access to the above and the beyond is *blocked.* There is no exit from the confines of this present world. The secular is all that we have. We must make our decisions, live our lives, make our plans, all within the closed arena of this time—the here and now.[1]

Each of us should understand that description instantly, because it is the viewpoint we are surrounded with every day of our lives and in every conceivable place and circumstance. Sadly, it is also an outlook we see reflected in our churches whenever we find ourselves aiming for immediate, visible success rather than trusting God while we do things in his way and await his invisible, spiritual blessings.

This is an outlook to which we must not be conformed. Instead of being conformed to this world, as if this world is all there is, we are to see all things as relating to God and eternity. Here is the contrast as expressed by Harry Blamires: "To think secularly is to think within a frame of reference bounded by the limits of our life on earth; it is to keep one's calculations rooted in this-worldly criteria. To think Christianly is to accept all things with the mind as related, directly or indirectly, to man's eternal destiny as the redeemed and chosen child of God."[2] If we are to have a modern reformation, we must learn to think Christianly.

HUMANISM: "YOU WILL BE LIKE GOD"

I have acknowledged that there is for Christians a proper concern for secular things, though secularism as a worldview is wrong. The same qualification holds for this next popular "ism," *humanism.*

Obviously, there is a proper kind of humanism, meaning a proper concern for human beings. Humanitarianism is a better word for it. People who care for other people are humanitarians. Christians should be humanitarians. However, there is also a *philosophical* humanism, a way of looking at people, particularly ourselves, apart from God, which is not right but is rather wrong and harmful. Instead of looking at people as creatures made in the image of God whom we should love and for whom we should care, humanism looks at man as the center of everything, which is an essentially secular point of view. This is why we often couple the adjective to the noun and speak more fully not just of humanism but of "secular humanism."

The best example of secular humanism is in the book of Daniel. One day Nebuchadnezzar, the king of Babylon, was on the roof of his palace looking out over his splendid hanging gardens to the prosperous city beyond. He was impressed with his handiwork and said, "Is not this the great Babylon I have built as the royal residence, by my mighty power and for the glory of my majesty?" (Dan. 4:30). It was a statement that everything he saw was "of" him, "by" him, and "for" his glory, which is what humanism is about. Humanism says that everything revolves around man and is for man's glory.

God would not tolerate this arrogance. So he judged Nebuchadnezzar with insanity, indicating that this is an insane philosophy. Nebuchadnezzar was driven out to live with the beasts and even acted like a beast until at last he acknowledged that God alone is the true ruler of the universe and that everything exists for God's glory and not ours. He said,

> "I, Nebuchadnezzar, raised my eyes toward heaven, and my sanity was restored. Then I praised the Most High; I honored and glorified him who lives forever.

"His dominion is an eternal dominion;
　his kingdom endures from generation to generation.
All the peoples of the earth are regarded as nothing.
He does as he pleases with the powers of heaven
　and the peoples of the earth.
No one can hold back his hand
　or say to him: 'What have you done?'" (vv. 34-35).

Humanism is opposed to God and is hostile to Christianity. This has always been so, but it is especially evident in the public statements of modern humanism: *A Humanist Manifesto* (1933), *Humanist Manifesto II* (1973), and *A Secular Humanist Declaration* (1980). The first of these, the 1933 document, said, "Traditional theism, especially faith in the prayer-hearing God, assumed to love and care for persons, to hear and understand their prayers, and to be able to do something about them, is an unproved and outmoded faith. Salvationism, based on mere affirmation, still appears as harmful, diverting people with false hopes of heaven hereafter. Reasonable minds look to other means for survival."[3]

The 1973 *Humanist Manifesto II* said, "We find insufficient evidence for belief in the existence of a supernatural," and, "There is no credible evidence that life survives the death of the body."[4]

Where does humanism lead? It leads to a deification of self and, contrary to what it professes, to a growing disregard for other people. For if there is no God, the self must be worshiped in God's place. In deifying self, humanism actually deifies nearly everything but God. Several years ago Herbert Schlossberg, one of the project directors for the Fieldstead Institute, wrote a book titled *Idols for Destruction* in which he showed how humanism has made a god of history, money, nature, power, religion, and, of course, humanity itself.[5] As far as disregarding other people, consider the bestsellers of the 1970s. You find titles such as *Winning through Intimidation* and *Looking Out for Number One*. These books say, in a manner utterly consistent with secular humanism, "Forget about other people; look out for yourself; *you* are what matters." What emerged in those years is what social critic Thomas Wolfe called "the Me

Decade" (the 1970s) and later, in the 1980s, what others saw as the golden age of greed.

Concerning humanism as well as secularism, the word for Christians is "do not conform any longer." Do not put yourself at the center. Do not worship the golden calf. Remember that the first expression of humanism was not the *Humanist Manifesto* of 1933 or even the arrogant words of Nebuchadnezzar, spoken about six hundred years before Christ, but the words of Satan, who told Eve in the Garden of Eden, "You will be like God, knowing good and evil" (Gen. 3:5).

RELATIVISM: "A MORAL MORASS"

We also need to consider *relativism*. Relativism means that there is no God and therefore no absolutes in any area of life. Everything is up for grabs. In chapter 1, we took note of Allan Bloom's *The Closing of the American Mind*, in which he makes this point. On the very first page of that book Bloom wrote, "There is one thing a professor can be absolutely certain of: almost every student entering the university believes, or says he believes, that truth is relative."[6]

What that book set out to prove is that education is impossible in such a climate. People can learn skills, of course. The student can learn to drive a truck, work a computer, handle financial transactions, and manage scores of other difficult things. But genuine education, which involves learning to sift through error to discover what is true rather than false, good rather than evil, and beautiful rather than ugly, is impossible, because the goals of real education—truth, goodness, and beauty—do not exist according to relativism. Besides, even if truth, goodness, and beauty did exist in some far-off metaphysical never-never-land, it would be impossible to find them, because even the process of discovering absolutes requires a belief in absolutes—it requires belief in such absolutes as the laws of logic, for example.

The solution Bloom offers in this otherwise excellent book is inadequate. He offers a return to Platonism, the classical Greek quest for absolutes, without acknowledging the need for a starting point in God and revelation. Nevertheless, Bloom is entirely right about what relativism does. It makes true education impossible and undermines even a quest for what is excellent.

Is it any wonder that, with such an underlying destructive philosophy as relativism, not to mention secularism and humanism, America is experiencing what *Time* magazine called "a moral morass" and "a values vacuum."[7]

MATERIALISM: "THE MATERIAL GIRL"

A fourth "ism" which is part of the "pattern of this world" is *materialism*. This takes us back to secularism, since it is a part of what secularism is. If "the cosmos is all there is or ever was or ever will be," then nothing exists but what is material or measurable, and if there is any value to be found in life, it must be in material terms. Be as healthy as you can. Live as long as you can. Get as rich as you can.

When today's young people are asked who their heroes or heroines are, what comes out rather quickly is that they have no people they actually look up to except possibly the rich and the famous—people like Michael Jackson and Madonna. And speaking of Madonna, isn't it interesting that she is often referred to as "the material girl"? For some fans, Madonna apparently represents the material things of this world—clothes, money, fame, and above all, pleasure. This is what today's young people want to be like! They want to be rich and famous and to have things and enjoy them. They want to be like Madonna.

Are evangelicals much different? The older ones probably would not know a Madonna song if they heard it, but they might well be equally materialistic. Are they any different from those the poet T. S. Eliot, in his poem "The Rock," described in this devastating epitaph?

> "Here were a decent godless people:
> Their only monument the asphalt road
> And a thousand lost golf balls."[8]

How different is the Lord Jesus Christ! He was born into a poor family, was placed in a borrowed manger at his birth, never had a home or a bank account or a family of his own. He said of himself, "Foxes have holes and birds of the air have nests, but the Son of Man has no place to lay his head" (Matt. 8:20). At his trial before Pilate he said, "My kingdom is not of this world. If it were, my servants would fight. . . . My kingdom is from another place" (John 18:36). When he died he was laid in a borrowed tomb. If there was ever a person who operated on the basis of values above and beyond the world in which we live, it was Jesus Christ. He was the polar opposite of "the material girl." But at the same time no one has ever affected this world for good as much as Jesus Christ has. It is into his image that we are to be transformed rather than being forced into the mold of this world's sinful and destructive "isms."

PRAGMATISM: "IT WORKS FOR ME"

The fifth "ism" that has formed contemporary culture as we know it is pragmatism, a philosophy that measures truth by its utilitarian value. It is probably safe to say that nothing is more characteristic of American thought and life than pragmatism.

This way of thinking has its roots in the philosophy of men such as John Stuart Mill (1806–1873), the British economist and social theorist whose ideas exercised a formative influence over many early American thinkers; John Dewey (1859–1952), who applied pragmatic standards to education; and William James (1842–1910), who applied the same system of thought to religion. James attended Princeton Theological Seminary as a young man but rebelled against the doctrinaire teaching he found there and later argued that the only way to determine the truth of anything is by its practical results. He is best known for his Lowell Lectures of 1906, published as *Pragmatism: A New Name for Old Ways of Thinking*,[9] and an earlier work, *The Varieties of Religious Experience*.[10]

However, the chief force behind the triumph of pragmatism in the West, particularly in the United States, was not philosophy but the Industrial Revolution. The goal of industrial pragmatism is efficiency leading to low cost, rather than quality, craftsmanship, or aesthetics. The goal is to find the fastest, least expensive way of producing products and getting things done. Pragmatism has improved living standards for millions who now enjoy the benefits of home ownership, adequate clothing, indoor plumbing, prescription drugs, cars, refrigerators, washing machines, television sets, and abundant food. But this has been achieved at significant cost! Items have become cheaper and more available, but they also tend to look alike. Quantity has marginalized quality, volume has smothered craftsmanship, and affordability has sabotaged beauty. The most prominent symbols of the modern industrial age and its pragmatism are skyscrapers, whose soaring steel and glass frames overshadow the towering spires of the cathedrals and churches that were there before them in nearly all our large cities.

Pragmatism has also had a powerful influence on American religion, as Michael Horton shows in *Made in America: The Shaping of Modern American Evangelicalism*,[11] a study of the unique features of American Christianity. William James taught that the only valid test of truthfulness in religion is whether religion works. "On pragmatic principles, if the hypothesis of God works satisfactorily in the widest sense of the word, it is true," James argued.[12] That is the way many evangelicals approach the Christian faith today, according to Horton. The claim "it works for me" seems to justify almost any belief, quite apart from a biblical foundation. As far as evangelism and church growth strategies are concerned, anything will be justified as long as it brings people into mass meetings or the church.

Perhaps the worst form of modern pragmatic Christianity is the approach of the faith healers who promise health, wealth, and happiness if their adherents only employ the right techniques. Pat Robertson urges Christians to employ the "laws of prosperity," to which, he seems to claim, God is bound. "It's a bit like tuning into a radio or television station" he says. "You get on the right frequency and you pick up the program."[13]

Horton analyzes this rightly when he says:

> While there is a great deal of mysticism among modern faith healers, they actually eliminate mystery from miracle, making healing predictable and, in fact, inevitable (naturalistic). No longer is a miracle the spontaneous and surprising work of God, but the right use of means, as predictable as any other scientific law. When God heals, it is not an interruption of natural laws. At its core, the faith healers proclaim a naturalistic faith. Salvation and healing are both human achievements.[14]

That is a strange development for fundamentalist Christianity, which is supposed to believe in the supernatural. But it is not actually so strange in light of the vast sea of cultural pragmatism in which all Americans, like fish, seem to live, move, and have their being.

MINDLESSNESS: "AMUSING OURSELVES TO DEATH"

When we think of the philosophies that determine the world we live in, we think first of those I have described: secularism, humanism, relativism, materialism, and pragmatism. But there is another cultural reality that may be even more significant for most of us than those philosophies. It is what I call "mindlessness," the inability or unwillingness to look at life in a thoughtful way. Since we are called to "mind renewal"—"Do not conform any longer to the pattern of this world, but be transformed *by the renewing of your mind*" (Rom. 12:2)—our present cultural mindlessness must be part of the "pattern of this world" that we are to recognize, engage, and overcome.

There are a number of causes for our mindlessness, including some of the things I mentioned earlier—Western materialism, the fast pace of modern life, and philosophical skepticism, among others. We will not think much if all we are concerned about is earning money. We will not think deeply if we are rushing around madly all the time and are too busy to think. We will not think at all if we do not believe thinking is worthwhile. These are important factors contributing to the present climate. But I want to suggest here, as I have in other places,[15] that the chief cause of our mindlessness is television.

What is wrong with television? It is not primarily that it short-ens attention spans, though it certainly does that. Nor is it chiefly that television glorifies violence and hypes immorality, though it does that too. The chief problem with television is that, for those who watch it consistently, it undermines and eventually destroys the ability to think. This is because it communicates primarily by images, not by words, and words are necessary if we are to perceive logical connections and make judgments as to what is right and what is wrong. An image cannot be true or false. Images just *are.* Although images can tell a story or establish a mood, they cannot make an argument.

Kenneth A. Myers, founder and editor of the Mars Hill Audio Tapes, has written a book titled *All God's Children and Blue Suede Shoes* in which he demonstrates the limits and failures of television by showing how the medium is unable to communicate even the simplest propositional sentences. He suggests these seven sen-tences as a test:

1. The cat is on the mat.
2. The cat is not on the mat.
3. The cat was on the mat.
4. The cat likes to be on the mat.
5. The cat should not be on the mat.
6. Get off the mat, cat!
7. If the cat doesn't get off the mat, I shall kick it.

There is nothing complex about these sentences. They progress from . . .

1. a plain factual statement, to
2. a parallel negative statement,
3. a statement about the past,
4. a statement of desire,
5. a statement of right versus wrong,
6. an imperative,
7. and a final statement projecting a future hypothetical condition.

We use statements such as these all the time. But as Myers points out, only the first could be presented visually, and even then with uncertainty. We might show a picture of a cat on a mat, but depending on how interesting the cat was, we might react to the cat alone and not notice the mat or the fact that the cat is "on" it at all. Indeed, as Myers says, even the simple verb "is" would probably be missing in any description we might give. We would not tend to say that the cat "is" anything.

And it gets harder after that. How would you "image" the negative (statement number 2)? Would a cat next to a mat do it? Or a picture of a cat on a mat followed by a picture of a cat next to a mat? We might react to pictures like those by saying, "The cat moved off the mat," since images, especially in television or in movies, suggest motion. But the simple negative—"the cat is not on the mat"—would probably escape us.

It is even more impossible to convey desire ("the cat likes to be on the mat") or a condition that should not be ("the cat should not be on the mat") or an imperative ("get off the mat, cat!") or a future hypothetical condition ("if the cat doesn't get off the mat, I shall kick it"). Myers says, "Television discourages reflection, tells us what we already know, relies on instant accessibility, reminds us of something else, and reflects the desires of the self."[16] But it does not develop great minds. Instead it is forming people who are incapable of any meaningful thought about anything, especially the claims of Christianity.

Another very helpful analysis of the nature of television is a book by Neil Postman, professor of communication arts and sciences at New York University, titled *Amusing Ourselves to Death: Public Discourse in the Age of Show Business.*[17] The first half of this book is a study of the difference between what Postman calls "the age of typography" and our present television age, which he calls "the age of show business." Typography refers to words in print. It concerns the communication of ideas by newspapers, pamphlets, and books. It is rational and analytic, because that is the way written words work. The age of show business is the image world that television has created.

When we read something that requires us to think, there is distance between ourselves and the printed page. We are not necessarily swept along by the words. We can analyze, ponder, weigh, compare, contrast, and disagree. We can reread a paragraph if we do not understand the argument. We may look up vocabulary we do not know. We may challenge the conclusions. Because there is a distance between ourselves and written words, we do not cheer a well-written sentence or applaud a powerful paragraph, though we may appreciate how well the work is done. Written words promote thinking. Moreover, the better people read and the more they read, the better and longer they can think.

Postman illustrates the strength of typography by the attention given to the famous debates about the political issues of the mid-1800s between Abraham Lincoln and Stephen Douglas. Those debates were held in public fairgrounds. They lasted six or seven hours, and after the debates were over the reporters sent the essence of the arguments over the telegraph to the newspapers, in which they were read and discussed by people everywhere the next morning. In those days, people were able to hear, understand, and form opinions about such complex issues as slavery, the authority and limits of federal government, and states' rights because their minds had been nurtured by the printed page. Unfortunately, television does not operate by or foster rational communication, which is why we are becoming an increasingly mindless culture.

What does television give us? It gives us entertainment, amusement, or diversion. We should remember that "amuse" is composed of two words: "a," meaning "not" (the negative), and "muse," meaning "to think." In other words, television is not only mindless; it is teaching us to be mindless too.

THE CULTURE COMES TO CHURCH

What is so significant about these philosophies is that they are having a strong and damaging influence on the church, particularly on its ministers and their approach to ministry. Romans 12:1-2 tells us that we are not to be "conformed" to this world but instead are to be "transformed" by the renewal of our minds. Unfortunately, the exact opposite seems to be happening. So pervasive have these cultural influences been that Christians seem to be increasingly conformed to the world and its thinking rather than being renewed in their minds, beginning to live differently as a consequence, and eventually exerting a reforming or restraining impact on the world around them.

Here is how we have adapted to and embraced these philosophies:

1. *Secularism.* How can we preach when people no longer believe in God or anything other than what science is able to see, weigh, and measure—when people find "God-talk" meaningless? Today's answer is that we should avoid theology or anything else that would "turn off" the unsaved, and be as worldly as possible. So we have created mega-churches designed as theaters with stages on which upscale, challenging talks are presented and dramas acted out; and our music mimics the godless music of the world.

We have become common, like the culture around us. Douglas Jones and Douglas Wilson have written a book titled *Angels in the Architecture* in which they expose the triviality of modern culture, arguing that secular man has fallen between the two stools of classical achievement on the one hand and Christian achievement on the other. "He cannot have the Nike of Samothrace, and he cannot have Bach's Mass in B Minor. He cannot have Virgil and he cannot have Milton. But he can hang a toilet seat on the gallery wall and apply for federal grants."[18] So much for unbelievers. But have evangelicals not fallen into the identical chasm? In an earlier age Christians wrote fine concertos and built inspiring cathedrals. But not today. "As it is, we are content with thumping on the guitar like a million other aspiring artists headed for Nashville, and we erect crystal cathedrals which look like an upscale gas works," claim these perceptive authors.[19]

2. *Humanism.* What should we talk about if not God or the soul or eternal life or judgment or salvation? Many answer that we must make *mankind* the substance of our message. So we have fostered "felt need" preaching in which the "audience" is instructed how to

overcome failure, grief, or depression, raise nice families, be happy, and enjoy terrific sex—but not how to get right with an offended God. We teach people to ask "What's in it for me?" when they come to church, and to evaluate what they experience by that standard.

Robert Schuller, pastor of the Crystal Cathedral in Anaheim, California, not far from Disneyland, is a blatant example of this misguided response. He argues that "classical Reformed theology has erred in its insistence that theology be God-centered, not man-centered. It was appropriate for Luther and Calvin to think theo-centrically," he says, but now "the scales must tip the other way."[20] His "gospel" is about achieving self-esteem.

3. *Relativism*. Because our contemporaries no longer believe in truth or absolutes, we do not proclaim truth anymore. Instead, we "share." We base our words on our feelings or the feelings of our listeners. Religion has become privatized and personal. How we feel about something has become the measure of its worth.

Have you noticed that in our culture facts have become mere opinions, and opinions have become facts? This is why we are offered the results of so many public opinion polls while the actual facts are ignored. A factual statement is treated merely as someone's "opinion," something another expert is expected to refute, while what the majority of the people think about some subject is treated as important whether the people have any grounds for forming a sound judgment about the subject or not. We hear such statements as, "Thirty-seven percent of those polled today think the president is guilty," or, "Thirty-seven percent think he is *not* guilty." But the only meaningful question is: "Is he guilty or not?" And that is determined by hard evidence and not by people's passing whims.

Many Christians have fallen into this contemporary mindless mind-set, which they display whenever they speak of the gospel chiefly as "what it means to me" or "what it has done for me." True, we need, as individuals, to believe the gospel and follow Christ, but what *I* believe or feel is not the important thing. What matters are the facts. Who is Jesus? What did he do? Why did he do it? And what does that require of me as his disciple?

The Christian counter to relativism is absolute truth, the kind of truth that Paul commended in Philippians 4:8: "Whatever is true, whatever is noble, whatever is right, whatever is pure, whatever is lovely, whatever is admirable—if anything is excellent or praiseworthy—think about such things." In making this list, Paul deliberately chose pagan rather than Christian virtues. This is because the virtues themselves are universal absolutes. Paul is not telling us to reflect on what we *think* is lovely or what we *feel* is admirable, as if the measure of value depended on our personal assessment of it. He is appealing to moral and aesthetic *absolutes,* saying that it is our duty as Christians to seek out such virtues and to be formed by them.

4. *Materialism.* Because we live in a materialistic age in which everything is regarded as a product to be sold, we also try to sell the gospel. Church growth theorists hold seminars in which preachers are taught to think of the masses as their market and the gospel as something that needs to be attractively packaged to sell. And we have Christian trade conventions where the tackiest "Jesus" merchandise is huckstered. Michael Horton reacts to those conventions by saying that "we have made our sovereign Lord about as cheap as the hairbrush that has his name stamped on it."[21] Power sells. So we have books with titles like *Power for Living* and *Power Evangelism.* As I write this chapter our television screens are carrying commercials for a religious book titled *Power for Life.*

5. *Pragmatism.* In response to pragmatism we have made "if it works" the only criterion for truth. Testimonies to business success, marriages turned around, and depression overcome, as well as personal good feelings, are supposed to prove the truth of Christianity. There are three problems with this. First, a Christianity like this is no longer unique among religions, since every religion promises practical, pragmatic benefits. Second, promises of success and happiness do not always work. Christianity does not always ensure good health or provide a comfortable way of life. Third, pragmatic Christianity shifts our thinking away from God to ourselves, which is a miserable place to be focused. Horton says:

In many ways, Christianity doesn't work. It has ruined some
crafty businessmen like Zacchaeus, who, by becoming a
Christian, ended up giving half his estate to the poor and paying back those he had cheated four times the amount he had
stolen. . . .

I'm not even sure that Christianity works if the goal is happiness. There are deeply satisfying feelings I have of being
secure, at peace, close to God. But there are also deeply troubling feelings. There are deeply disturbing times of wrestling
with a God who reveals himself as someone other than the
God I would like to worship. And there are times when the
gospel's implications force me to enter a period of intense
internal struggle. I remember hearing preachers say that non-
Christians are unhappy and unfulfilled, while Christians are
"victorious" and "happy in the Lord." But that isn't always
true. I know non-Christians who are very happy. In fact, it is
their contentedness which leads them to avoid discussions of
religion. They don't think they need it.

If we seek to justify Christianity on pragmatic grounds,
ours will continue to be just another self-help, self-improve-
ment program.[22]

6. *Mindlessness*. We live in a rapidly changing world, and one of
the indicators of the turbulence is that we are constantly inventing
new words to describe what is happening. One of the new words I
have noticed recently is "factoid." It appears regularly on CNN news
programs to mark a break between segments, introducing a "fact"
that is unrelated to anything else on the news program itself or in
the viewer's mind. It doesn't signify anything. It is just . . . well, a
fact. But a short one, hence, a "factoid."

It strikes me that this is an apt word to describe much of what
passes for learning in our mindless, disconnected age. It is a small
capsule of what was troubling Neil Postman when he described
television news as entertainment. He wrote, "We are presented not
only with fragmented news but news without context, without
consequences, without value, and therefore without essential seriousness; that is to say, news as pure entertainment."[23]

What does one do with "factoids" in an entertainment-focused age? The answer is: Turn them into a game, which is why we have *Trivial Pursuit. Trivial Pursuit* is a game of myriad facts about all sorts of things, but none of the facts have significance. They serve only to amuse us for a moment. But Christianity is not a game. It is a serious rather than a trivial pursuit. When we treat it as entertainment we destroy it.

In Neil Postman's chapter on religion in *Amusing Ourselves to Death* he asks what happens when church appears on television? The chief loss is a sense of the transcendent, Postman says, "Everything that makes religion an historic, profound and sacred human activity is stripped away; there is no ritual, no dogma, no tradition, no theology, and above all, no sense of spiritual transcendence. On these shows, the preacher is tops. God comes out as second banana."[24] And later he says, "If I am not mistaken, the word for this is blasphemy."[25]

Sadly, the dominance of television in our culture has had its impact on the churches and on preaching, where the services are now increasingly designed to be entertaining and the preachers are told to win people by helping them to have a good time.

Not all American religion is like this. But much is, and even the best is influenced to an astonishing degree by these ideas. It should be said of such religion—as God does indeed say of it—that it has "a form of godliness" but is "denying its power" (2 Tim. 3:5). Pagan religion can be advanced by worldly devices. But true Christianity is created by the power of God alone and grows strong only as those who have been brought to faith are transformed from within by the "renewing" of their minds (Rom. 12:2).

YOUR MIND MATTERS

The bottom line of these observations is that many churches of our day, particularly evangelical ones, have become worldly, and that what they most need to do is begin thinking about and rediscovering the theology of the Bible. Moreover, they need to do it in conscious opposition to the secularism, humanism, relativism, materialism, pragmatism, and mindlessness of our declining culture.

Romans 12:1-2, which I used as a jumping-off place for this chapter, contains a contrast between the negative idea of not being "conformed" and the positive challenge to be "transformed" by the renewing of our minds. Conformity is something that happens to us outwardly. Transformation happens inwardly. We can see this when we realize that the Greek word translated "transformed" is *metamorpho*, from which we get the English word *metamorphosis*. It is what happens to a caterpillar when it turns into a butterfly.

And there is this interesting fact: This Greek word *metamorpho* is found four times in the New Testament: once in Romans 12:2 and once in 2 Corinthians 3:18, to describe our being transformed into the likeness of Jesus Christ; and twice in the Gospels to describe the change that took place in Jesus on the Mount of Transfiguration. Those verses say, "There he was *transfigured* before them" (Matt. 17:2; Mark 9:2). It is striking that the word used by Paul to describe our transformation by the renewing of our minds, so that we will not be conformed to this world, is used by the evangelists to describe the transfiguration of Jesus from the form of his earthly humiliation to the radiance that the disciples were privileged to witness on the mountain! It is a way of saying that we are to become like Jesus by this inner transformation. We are to be changed into his glorious character and likeness.

Paul writes about this transformation in 2 Corinthians, saying, "we, who with unveiled faces all reflect the Lord's glory, are being transformed into his likeness with ever-increasingly glory, which comes from the Lord, who is the Spirit" (2 Cor. 3:18).

In 2 Corinthians Paul says, "It is happening." In Romans 12 he says, "Let it happen," thereby putting the responsibility, though not the power to accomplish the transformation, upon us. How does it happen? It happens by the renewing of our minds, and the way our minds become renewed is by study of the life-giving and renewing Word of God. Without that study we will remain in the world's mold, unable to think as Christians and therefore also unable to act as Christians. We will be Christians in name and by profession, but we will be worldly, unbelieving people in all other respects. By contrast, as a result of that study, blessed and empowered by the Holy

Spirit, we will begin to take on something of the glorious luster of the Lord Jesus Christ and will become increasingly like him.

That is what I want to see happen as a result of coming to understand the doctrines of Christianity that were the heart of the Reformation and are the subject of the following chapters: "Scripture alone" (*sola Scriptura*), "Christ alone" (*solus Christus*), "grace alone" (*sola gratia*), "faith alone" (*sola fide*), and "glory to God alone" (*soli Deo gloria*). In the second section of this book, we will study each of those five doctrines carefully, thinking about what they mean and considering why they are important. In the final section, we will explore how an understanding and application of these doctrines will transform our worship and refocus our lives.

Part Two

DOCTRINES
THAT SHOOK
THE WORLD

Scripture Alone

When God from heaven gave his Word
His Word was all-sufficient;
It needs no words I may have heard
To add to or be in it.
So I will take God's Book and read,
To learn what God desires;
The Bible gives the strength I need
To do what God requires.

I would like to see the beginning of a new reformation in our day, and I hope you would like to see it too and are praying for it. I hope you have become nauseated with the tawdry entertainment that passes for the true worship of God in many of our churches and, like the saints of the past, are longing for more of the deep truths of the inerrant Word of God. We certainly need a reformation. But what I am suggesting in this book is that, although we need to recapture the great theological truths that underlay and fueled the sixteenth-century Reformation, the form that recovery will have to take in our day must vary from the sixteenth-century because the battle lines have shifted and the specific issues have changed.

When we think of the Reformation we think naturally of the five great theses of that movement: *sola Scriptura, solus Christus, sola gratia, sola fide,* and *soli deo gloria.* Those doctrines are exactly what we need to rediscover. But to do so we need to relate them to the specific challenges of our time, not only to those of the sixteenth century.

In Martin Luther's day, *sola Scriptura* had to do with the Bible being the sole ultimate authority for Christians over against challenges to it from the traditions of the medieval church, church councils, and the pope. The Reformers wanted Scripture to stand alone as the church's true authority. Today, at least in the evangelical church, that is not our chief problem; we assert biblical authority. Rather, our problem is in deciding whether the Bible is *sufficient* for the church's life and work. We confess its authority, but we discount its ability to do what is necessary to draw unbelievers to Christ, enable us to grow in godliness, provide direction for our lives, and transform and revitalize society. So we substitute such things as Madison Avenue methodology for biblical evangelism, special "religious" experiences rather than knowledge of the Word to promote and guarantee sanctification, special revelations for discerning the will of God for our lives, and a trust in the power of votes and money to change society. In other words, in the sixteenth century the battle was against those who wanted to add church traditions to Scripture, but in our day the battle is against those who would have us use worldly means to do God's work.

The battle lines have also shifted in regard to the doctrines of *solus Christus, sola gratia, sola fide,* and *soli deo gloria,* but we will come to them in later chapters.

A BIBLE-BASED MINISTRY

One of the blessings of serving Tenth Presbyterian Church, where I have been senior pastor for more than thirty years, is that for over the one hundred and seventy years of its long history (1829–) the church has stood for the authority and sufficiency of the Bible as the Word of God. The elders and most of the people believe the Bible to be the unique Word of God, the only infallible rule of faith and practice, and they want the Bible to be treasured and obeyed in all areas of the church's life.

This was true from the beginning. But it is illustrated by an incident from the early ministry of Donald Grey Barnhouse, one of my predecessors at Tenth Church (1927–1960) and a man who had a profound influence on my idea of what the ministry should be. A week or two after Barnhouse became pastor of Tenth Church, he entered the pulpit one Sunday morning and opened the pulpit Bible to a point near the middle, where he then placed his sermon notes, his Bible, and a hymn book. As he looked down he noticed that the words on the pages of the pulpit Bible were part of a curse upon those nations that do not know God, and it occurred to him that he would like to have before him a passage containing words of some great promise about Scripture. So he opened the Bible to Isaiah 55:10-11:

As the rain and the snow come down from heaven,
and do not return to it without watering the earth
and making it bud and flourish, so that it yields seed for
    the sower and bread for the eater,
so is my word that goes out from my mouth:
It will not return to me empty, but will accomplish
    what I desire
    and achieve the purpose for which I sent it.

To his surprise he discovered that for decades his predecessors had apparently done the same thing. The edges of the Bible were worn in half circles curving inward from the bindings at that text, and the pages were torn and mended. (Incidentally, that Bible can still be seen in the archives of Tenth Presbyterian Church.) As Barnhouse later observed, the pages "containing the great fifty-fifth chapter of Isaiah and the preceding page with the fifty-third chapter of Isaiah concerning the Lord Jesus Christ as God's Lamb, [gave] mute evidence that the men who have stood in the pulpit of Tenth Church for more than a century were men of the living Word and the written Word."[1]

Later Barnhouse discovered that Psalm 119 was similarly worn. Apparently, those who had preached from that pulpit, finding it difficult to keep their notes on the Isaiah pages, looked for another passage that would also remind them of the power and priority of God's Word. Barnhouse told this story in a booklet marking the twenty-fifth anniversary of his pastorate, concluding:

> It is my prayer that no man shall ever stand in this pulpit as long as time shall last who does not desire to have all that he does based upon this Book. For this Book does not *contain* the Word of God, it is the Word of God. And though we may preach the Word with all the stammering limitations of our human nature, the grace of God does the miracle of the ministry, and through human lips speaks the divine Word, and the hearts of the people are refreshed. There is no other explanation for the continuing power of a church that is poorly located, that is without endowment, but which continues to draw men and women to the capacity of its seating arrangements, morning and evening, summer and winter, and which sends its sons and daughters by the score to preach the unsearchable riches of Christ throughout the world.[2]

THE INERRANCY OF GOD'S WORD

About ten years into my pastorate, at the end of 1977 and the beginning of 1978, I helped start an organization that was concerned with the important matter we perceived to be under attack at that time, namely, the Bible's inerrancy. Our organization was called the International Council on Biblical Inerrancy, and it had within it such evangelical leaders as Francis Schaeffer, J. I. Packer, A. Wetherell Johnson, R. C. Sproul, John Gerstner, and Roger Nicole. It had as its purpose the task of "elucidating, vindicating and applying the doctrine of biblical inerrancy as an essential element for the authority of Scripture and a necessity for the health of the church of God."

We held three scholarly gatherings to hammer out three documents of "affirmation and denial." The first, quite naturally, was on inerrancy ("The Chicago Statement on Biblical Inerrancy").[3] The second was on sound principles of biblical interpretation ("The Chicago Statement on Biblical Hermeneutics").[4] The third dealt with Bible application ("The Chicago Statement on Biblical

Application").[5] We also held two large lay conferences, the first in San Diego in the spring of 1982 and the second in Washington in the fall of 1988.

In the early days we were often asked why inerrancy was important. "Isn't it enough to believe that the Bible is trustworthy in the areas of faith and morals?" people asked. It is not that simple. The Bible is a historical book and Christianity is a historical religion. So if the Bible errs in matters of historical fact, Christianity will inevitably be affected. A hundred years of German "historical Jesus" research proved that. The scholars involved in that effort wanted to separate the "Christ of faith" from the "Jesus of history" in hopes of finding out who the true Jesus was. But as Albert Schweitzer proved in *The Quest of the Historical Jesus*,[6] all these scholars succeeded in doing was making Jesus over into their own images. Rationalists produced a rationalist Jesus, socialists a socialistic Jesus, moralists a moralist Jesus, and so on. The attempt to have Christianity without its historical base was a failure.

Besides, if part of the Bible is true and part is not, who is to tell us which parts are the true parts? Either we must make the decision ourselves, in which case truth becomes subjective, or else the scholars must tell us what we can and cannot believe. Fortunately God has not left us either to our own whims or to the whims of scholars.

I wrestled with the inerrancy of the Bible during my seminary years. It is not that I questioned it. My problem was that my teachers did not believe this, and much of what I was hearing in the classroom was meant to reveal the Bible's errors so that students would not depend on it too deeply. What was a student to do? The professors seemed to have all the facts. How were professors to be challenged when they argued that recent scholarship had shown that the old, simplistic views about the Bible being inerrant were no longer valid and that therefore we should admit that the Bible is filled with errors?

As I worked on this I discovered some interesting things. First, the problems imagined to be in the Bible were hardly new problems. For the most part those problems were known centuries ago, even by such ancient theologians as Augustine and Jerome, who discussed apparent contradictions in their substantial correspondence.

I also discovered that the results of sound scholarship have *not* tended to uncover more and more problems, as my professors were suggesting, still less disclose more and more "errors." Rather they have tended to *resolve* problems and to show that what were once thought to be errors are not errors at all.

Second Kings 15:29 speaks of a king of Assyria named Tiglath-Pileser. He is said to have conquered the Israelites of the northern kingdom and to have taken many of them into captivity. A generation ago liberal scholars were saying that this king never existed because there was no independent record of him, and that the fall of the northern kingdom to Assyria was mythology. But then archaeologists excavated Tiglath-Pileser's capital city and found his name pressed into bricks which read: "I, Tiglath-Pileser, king of Assyria, . . . am a conqueror from the Great Sea which is in the country of Amurru as far as the Great Sea which is in the Nairi country," that is, the Mediterranean. In other words, archaeologists have found evidence not only of Tiglath-Pileser's existence but even of the very campaign 2 Kings describes. The English reader can find the king's account of his battles in James B. Pritchard's *Ancient Near Eastern Texts Relating to the Old Testament*.[7]

A generation ago some scholars were arguing that Moses could not have written the first five books of the Old Testament because writing was not known in Moses' day. That seemed irrefutable enough. If writing was not known in Moses' day, Moses could not have known how to write, and if Moses did not know how to write, he could not have written the Pentateuch. But in this case, it was the underlying premise that was wrong. As it turns out, not only was writing known in Moses' day, there were actually many written languages. Today we know of at least six different languages from the very area of the world in which Moses led the Israelites for forty years.

Here is my favorite example: At the end of 1974 *Time* magazine ran a cover story titled "How True Is the Bible?" It surveyed the liberal attacks on the Bible's reliability and concluded, somewhat as I did after my study of what the evidence in this area has proved, that the credibility of the Bible has actually grown in recent decades. *Time* wrote:

> The breadth, sophistication and diversity of all this biblical investigation are impressive, but it begs a question: Has it made the Bible more credible or less? Literalists who feel the ground move when a verse is challenged would have to say that credibility has suffered. Doubt has been sown, faith is in jeopardy. But believers who expect something else from the Bible may well conclude that its credibility has been enhanced. After more than two centuries of facing the heaviest scientific guns that could be brought to bear, the Bible has survived—and is perhaps the better for the siege. Even on the critics' own terms—historical fact—the Scriptures seem more acceptable now than they did when the rationalists began the attack.[8]

I found it interesting and important that the Bible was being defended by a secular magazine and that it was doing so better than even some so-called preachers and scholars. But two weeks later there were strong critical letters from Martin Marty, a regular writer for *The Christian Century*, and Harvey Cox, a professor at the Harvard Divinity School. Marty began his letter by saying, "The faith of your Bible believers is the opposite of biblical faith!" *Time* had published a balanced article. It had not suggested that the Bible was inerrant or even authoritative, only that it was historically reliable, and the two scholars could not even stand to have it called reliable!

The letters were on page 38. But when I got to page 65 I found a report in the science section of an archaeological expedition in the southern area of the Sinai peninsula under the direction of a Jewish archaeologist named Beno Rothenberg. Rothenberg had been working at a place called "Solomon's mines," because an ancient smelting operation had been there and he wanted to find out if the area had really been worked by Jews and if it was a place where they might have melted down the gold used in the construction of

Solomon's great temple. He had discovered that the area in fact had been occupied by Jewish workmen in the days of Solomon and that it may indeed have been where the temple gold had been smelted. But that was not all. Rothenberg had pushed back through the strata at the site and discovered that this ancient foundry had been developed originally by the Midianites. *Time* knew that few of its readers would know who the Midianites were. So the writer explained, " . . . the Midianites, a little-known people who dwelled in the area and are identified in Genesis as the first metal workers . . ."[9]

At that point I began to laugh because, although there may have been many places where that little bit of Bible verification could have appeared, it had appeared in the very issue in which the liberal scholars were saying, "The faith of your Bible believers is the opposite of biblical faith!"

I thought, the Holy Spirit seems to have a sense of humor!

THE SUFFICIENCY OF GOD'S WORD

To underscore a point made earlier, however, inerrancy is not the most critical issue facing the church today. The most serious issue, I believe, is the Bible's *sufficiency.* Do we believe that God has given us what we need in this book? Or do we suppose that we have to supplement the Bible with human things? Do we need sociological techniques to do evangelism, pop psychology and pop psychiatry for Christian growth, extra-biblical signs or miracles for guidance, or political tools for achieving social progress and reform?

It is possible to believe that the Bible is the inerrant Word of God, the only infallible rule of faith and practice, and yet to neglect it and effectually repudiate it just because we think that it is not sufficient for today's tasks and that other things need to be brought in to accomplish what is needed. This is exactly what many evangelicals and evangelical churches are doing.

The Bible's sufficiency is the point of what are perhaps its three most important passages about itself: Psalm 19; Matthew 4; and 2 Timothy 3. The first contrasts the written Word with God's general revelation. The second shows how Jesus used the Bible to overcome temptation. The third is Paul's advice to Timothy in view of the terrible times he saw coming. Each stresses that the Word of God alone is sufficient for these challenges.

The first part of Psalm 19 is about the revelation of God in nature; the second part is about the Bible:

> The law of the LORD is *perfect,*
>> reviving the soul.
> The statues of the LORD are *trustworthy,*
>> making wise the simple.
> The precepts of the LORD are *right,*
>> giving joy to the heart.
> The commands of the LORD are *radiant,*
>> giving light to the eyes.
> The fear of the LORD is *pure,*
>> enduring forever.
> The ordinances of the LORD are *sure*
>> and altogether righteous.
> They are more *precious* than gold,
>> than much pure gold;
> they are *sweeter* than honey,
>> than honey from the comb.
> By them is your servant *warned;*
>> in keeping them there is great *reward.*
> (vv. 7-11, emphasis added)

The revelation of God in nature is wonderful (vv. 1-6), but it is limited. By contrast, the revelation of God in Scripture is perfect, trustworthy, right, radiant, pure, sure, precious, sweet, and rewarding. By what language would it be possible for the psalmist more effectively to emphasize the complete and utter sufficiency of God's Word?

In Matthew 4 we discover the sufficiency of God's Word in temptation, for it was by quotations from Deuteronomy 8:3, 6:16, and 6:13 that Jesus withstood Satan. Jesus did not reason with Satan, though his powers of reason certainly surpassed those of the tempter. Jesus did not resort to supernatural power to escape this trial or somehow get rid of Satan, though he had that power as well.

He did not ask God for some special sign or angelic intervention to tell him what he was to say to Satan. The issue was far simpler than that. Jesus knew the Bible, stood on it, and used it forcefully.

Second Timothy 3 is the same. Paul is warning his young protégé against the terrible times coming in the last days. They will be days in which "people will be lovers of themselves, lovers of money, boastful, proud, abusive, disobedient to their parents, ungrateful, unholy, without love, unforgiving, slanderous, without self-control, brutal, not lovers of the good, treacherous, rash, conceited, lovers of pleasure rather than lovers of God" (vv. 2-4). This could refer to what we might call the very last days, that is, the days just before the second coming of Jesus Christ in judgment. But since Paul is instructing Timothy about what to do in the challenges *he* will face, he must be referring to the entire time between the Lord's first and second comings. In other words, this is a frightening description of the world in which we live, not only the very end times. And of course, it does describe our world. It describes it perfectly.

But here is the shocking thing: Having described this evil worldly culture by its vices, Paul adds in verse 5, "having a form of godliness but denying its power." A "form of godliness" cannot refer to pagans. Paul would never have described the pagans of his day as having "a form of godliness." He would have referred to their religions as multiple forms of ungodliness, as he does in the first chapter of Romans. If this cannot be describing pagans, it must be describing the church. In other words, the problem Paul is describing is not that the world will be evil in the final days before Christ's return but that the church will be like the world, as it is today. The church will be indistinguishable from the world and will be equally corrupt, at least when you look beneath the surface.

What is Timothy to do when such days come? Surely Paul must have some secret new weapon, some unexpected trick for him to use. No, instead of something new, we find Paul recommending what Timothy has had all along—the Word of God—because the Bible is sufficient even for terrible times like these. "But as for you, continue in what you have learned and have become convinced of, because you know those from whom you learned it, and how from infancy you have known the holy Scriptures, which are able to make you wise for salvation through faith in Christ Jesus" (2 Tim. 3:14-15).

Sufficient for Evangelism

The first thing the Word of God is sufficient for is evangelism. In fact, it is the only thing that really works in evangelism. Everything else—captivating music, moving testimonies, emotional appeals, even coming forward to make a personal commitment to Jesus Christ—all that is at best supplementary. And if such things are used or depended upon apart from the faithful preaching and teaching of God's Word, the "conversions" that result are spurious conversions, which is to say that those who respond become Christians in name only. The only way the Holy Spirit works to regenerate lost men and women is by the Bible. Peter said, "you have been born again, not of perishable seed, but of imperishable, through the living and enduring word of God" (1 Pet. 1:23).

The problem is that many people do not actually believe this and therefore they want to lean on other things. Some evangelists, such as Charles G. Finney, have depended on certain crusade techniques. Others, such as those in the Vineyard movement, look to "signs and wonders."

Consider, however, the example of Jesus Christ himself. Mark the evangelist introduces Jesus with these words: "After John was put in prison, Jesus went into Galilee, proclaiming the good news of God. 'The time has come,' he said. 'The kingdom of God is near. Repent and believe the good news!'" (Mark 1:14-15). He introduces Jesus as a preacher, and what Jesus is preaching is the gospel. For that is what the phrase "good news of God" means. The Good News is the gospel. Moreover, if we ask what this gospel is about, the answer is that it is about the kingdom of God. God's kingdom has come near because Jesus is near. The gospel is about his kingdom. If we also ask, "What does that have to do with me?" or "How do I become a part of this kingdom?" the answer is, "Repent and believe the good news." That is exactly what we tell people to do today. They must repent of their sin and believe the gospel of God's salvation from sin in Jesus Christ.

A little further on Mark tells how Jesus went into the synagogue at Capernaum on the Sabbath and began to teach there. The paragraph tells how Jesus "began to *teach*," how "the people were amazed at his *teaching*, because he *taught* them as one who had authority," and how they were astonished, asking, "'What is this? A new *teaching*—and with authority!'" (Mark 1:21, 22, 27). By this time we should be getting Mark's point. Jesus has come as a preacher, and what he is preaching is God's Word.

Next, in Mark's account, Peter's mother-in-law got sick. She had a fever, which was a serious matter in the days before aspirin and antibiotics. More people died from fever in past days than from any other single cause. Jesus was told about it, and he came to the house and healed this woman. He did it because he had the power to do it and because he cared.

As soon as word of the healing got out, many more people came to be healed, which is exactly what we might expect to have happened in a day when there was little medicine and many ineffective doctors. We are probably not far wrong to suppose that in a short while hundreds had gathered. Jesus healed them. Again, it was because he had the power to do so and because he cared for these people.

Evening came. It grew dark. Everyone went home to bed. But the next morning all these people were back, probably with others. This was wonderful, a teacher who could actually heal diseases. As soon as the disciples saw the large crowd they went looking for Jesus and were startled to find that he was not there. Where was he? Someone probably said, "I know where he is. He's out praying. That is what he does in the morning." When the disciples finally found Jesus, they exclaimed, "Everyone is looking for you!" (v. 37). They meant, "What are you doing here praying when there is such important work to do?"

If Peter had been the spokesman, I can imagine him explaining the situation to Jesus like this: "Jesus," he might have said, "I know you want to preach, and that you think prayer is important.

So do we. You have taught us that. But I want to point out something you may have missed: Yesterday morning, when you were teaching in the synagogue, you had a decent response. But there were only twenty people present. We counted them. However, in the afternoon, when you began to do these healings, hundreds responded. I think you have really hit upon it. You have found the key to doing successful evangelism. People like healings. So let's get back down there and heal some more people. If we keep this up, we will really bring in God's kingdom."

Jesus' reply to the disciples was a negative, though he did not actually use the word *no*. He said, "Let us go somewhere else—to the nearby villages—so I can preach there also. That is why I have come" (v. 38).

Isn't that striking? Jesus was refusing to carry on a healing ministry. Why? Had he lost his power? Didn't he care anymore? Of course not. Besides, he does other healings later on in the Gospel. Why did he refuse the disciple's challenge then? It is because he knew that if he allowed the miracles to eclipse the teaching, the countryside might soon be filled with thousands of fit and healthy people, but in spite of their good health they would all die eventually and perish in hell. If, on the other hand, he focused on teaching them the Bible, though many would have less than perfect health and there would still be many physical diseases, many of these people would also believe and those who did believe would go to heaven. Jesus saw things God's way, and he would not allow anything to deter him from his Father's business.

Besides, miracles convert no one, as becomes clear in the story of the rich man and Lazarus. According to the story, when both of these men died, Lazarus was carried into the presence of Abraham in paradise but the rich man went to hell. At first the rich man asked Abraham to send Lazarus to provide him some comfort. When that was said to be impossible, he asked that Lazarus be sent back to warn his brothers, since they were as wicked as he. "I beg you, father, send Lazarus to my father's house, for I have five brothers. Let him warn them, so that they will not also come to this place of torment" (Luke 16:27-28).

Abraham replied, "They have Moses and the Prophets; let them listen to them."

The rich man persisted, "No, father Abraham, . . . but if someone from the dead goes to them, they will repent."

Abraham's final word, the climactic point of the parable, was, "If they do not listen to Moses and the Prophets, they will not be convinced even if someone rises from the dead" (vv. 29-31). This shows explicitly that people are not converted by miracles, even by resurrections. On the contrary, the only thing that will ever regenerate anyone is the Holy Spirit operating through the preaching and teaching of God's Word.

This is also what Paul says in Romans 10:6-9. And it is what Moses was saying in the verses from Deuteronomy 30 that Paul quotes there: "The righteousness that is by faith says: 'Do not say in your heart, "Who will ascend into heaven?"' (that is, to bring Christ down) 'or "Who will descend into the deep?"' (that is, to bring Christ up from the dead). But what does it say? 'The word is near you; it is in your mouth and in your heart,' that is, the word of faith we are proclaiming: That if you confess with your mouth, 'Jesus is Lord,' and believe in your heart that God raised him from the dead, you will be saved."

The people had been given "Moses and the Prophets." That is the word which, according to Moses, was "near" them, in their mouths and hearts (Deut. 30:14). And that word was sufficient. Because if they did not heed that written word and repent of their sin and turn to God in faith on the basis of that given revelation, they would not be changed even by a religion of miracles. No number of "signs and wonders," however great, would save them.

Today, says Paul, in exactly the same way people have the Christian gospel, which is "the word of faith we are proclaiming." That gospel is here now, and because it is being proclaimed, all possible excuses for failing to believe in Christ and be saved from the coming judgment are eliminated.

During the decade I served as chairman of the International Council on Biblical Inerrancy (1978–1988) I listened to many sermons on the Bible, and one of the best I heard was by W. A.

Criswell, well-known pastor emeritus of the First Baptist Church of Dallas. He preached it at ICBI's first "Summit Meeting" in 1978. At the time Criswell had been in the ministry for more than fifty years, and he had been chosen to address this amazing gathering of 350 pastors, scholars, and leaders of the major parachurch organizations on the subject "What Happens When I Preach the Bible as Literally True?" His answer was a *tour de force,* as he explained what had happened to him, what had happened to his church, and what he believes happens to God when God's Word is thus used and honored.

About a year after he had gone to the Dallas church, Criswell had announced to his already well-established congregation that he was going to preach through the entire Bible, beginning with Genesis and going right on to the last benedictory prayer in Revelation. "You never heard such lugubrious prognostications," he reported. People said it would kill the church. Nobody would come to hear someone preach about Habakkuk, Haggai, and Nahum. Most people didn't even know who those biblical books or characters were, they said. Criswell pursued this plan all the same, and to everyone's astonishment the problem that developed was not the demise of the church but rather where to put all the people who were pressing in weekly to hear Criswell's consistent biblical preaching. There were thousand of conversions, and today the First Baptist Church of Dallas is one of the largest, most effective, and most biblically sound churches in the country.[10]

Scoffers abound. Critics multiply. There has always been opposition to the teaching of the Bible. But the lesson of history is the unique power of the Bible to regenerate lost sinners, transform their lives, and build churches.

Sufficient for Sanctification

Several years ago I completed a series of studies on Romans. It had occupied me for eight years. During that time I had discovered quite a few important things about Romans, but the most striking lesson I learned was the way the apostle Paul approached the subject of sanctification. It was striking because it is not what we might

expect or what many people today desire. When we think of sanctification today, most of us think of one or the other of two things.
Either we think of a method ("Here are three steps to sanctification;
do this and you will be holy"), or we think of an experience ("You
need a second work of grace, a baptism of the Holy Spirit," or something else). Paul's approach was to know the Bible and its teaching
about what has been done for us by God in our salvation.

Paul makes this clear in Romans 6, where he says, "In the same
way, count yourselves dead to sin but alive to God in Christ Jesus"
(v. 11). This is the first time in the letter that Paul tells his readers
to do something, and what they are to do is "count" or "reckon
upon" the fact that God has done an irreversible work in their lives
as a result of which they have died to sin (the verb is in the past
tense, an aorist) and have been made alive to God in Christ Jesus.
In other words, he is referring them back to the doctrine of the
believer's union with Christ which he had developed in detail in
chapter 5. Before, we were "in Adam"; now, we are "in Christ."
Before, we were under "condemnation"; now, we are "justified."
Before, we were perishing; now, we possess "eternal life."

Paul's "method" for sanctification is biblical doctrine. That is,
to live as Christians we must know what God has done to us in
making us Christians. We must know what has happened, and the
only way we can know what has happened is to know the Bible.
Then, because we know what God has done to us, we are to go on
with God, acting on the basis of what has been done for us and in
us. We can express it this way: We cannot go back to being what
we were before. We are new creatures in Christ. And if we are new
creatures in Christ, the only thing we can do is get on with living
the Christian life. In other words, there is no way for us to go but
forward.

Here is an illustration in the form of three questions:

First, can an adult become a child again? Clearly, the answer is
no. No one can reverse the aging process.

Second, can an adult act childish? We know the answer to that,
because we see it often. Of course, adults often act like children.

But now, here is the third critical question: What do you say to an adult who is acting childish? Women know the answer to that question because they say it to men all the time. They say, "For heaven's sake, just grow up!" That is exactly what Paul is saying to believers. "You are Christians now [if you really are]. You cannot go back to being what you were before. You cannot become 'unsaved.' So for heaven's sake, grow up and start acting like Christians."

This has nothing to do with either a method or an experience. It has everything to do with knowing and living by the sufficient Word of God. Is it not true that one reason we see such immature and even sinful behavior among Christians today is that they have not really been taught what God has done to them and for them when he saved them? And aren't our churches immature precisely because the pastors are not teaching Bible doctrines?

Sufficient for Guidance

Not long ago one of my staff gave me a script to be used for an imagined "evangelical psychiatric hotline," the kind of recorded message one might hear when he or she calls a participating church for psychiatric help. It went like this:

If you are *obsessive-compulsive*, please press 1 repeatedly.
If you are *codependent*, please ask someone else to press 2.
If you have *multiple personalities*, please press 3, 4, 5, and 6.
If you are *paranoid*, we know who you are and what you want.
   Just stay on the line so we can trace the call.
If you are an *evangelical*, listen carefully and a little voice will
   tell you which number to press.

Is that how we are to find guidance from God for our lives? A little voice? Not at all. That is a kind of mysticism. "I prayed about it, and God told me to do the following." In former days, a statement like that would be followed by a more mature believer asking for "chapter and verse," meaning, where do you find that in Scripture? We need to get rid of that way of talking and of such false claims.

God has given us all the guidance we need in the Bible. So if there is something we want or think we need that is not in the Bible—What job shall I take? Where shall I live? Whom shall I marry?—after having prayed for God's providential guidance, we are free to do whatever seems right to us, knowing that God who cares for us always will certainly keep us in his way. In areas about which the Bible does not speak explicitly, we are free to act as we think best, as long as we are obeying God and trying to live a godly life.

That does not mean that God does not have a plan for our lives in all areas. He does. He has a detailed plan for all things, having pre-ordained "whatsoever comes to pass," as the Westminster Confession of Faith says. But that does not mean that we have to *know* God's plan in advance. In fact, we cannot. But what we *can* know, and need to know, is what God has told us in the Bible.

What has God told us?

In Romans 8 God offers a pattern for what he is doing with us, which includes being delivered from judgment for our sin and from sin's power and being made increasingly like Jesus Christ. The five decisive steps of that plan are: 1) foreknowledge, 2) predestination, 3) effectual calling, 4) justification, and 5) glorification (vv. 29-30).

There are also many specific matters related to guidance—the Ten Commandments, for example. It is God's will that we have no other gods before him; that we do not worship him by the use of images; that we do not misuse his name; that we remember the Sabbath by keeping it holy; that we honor our parents; that we do not murder or commit adultery or steal or give false testimony or covet (cf. Ex. 20). Jesus amplified many of these commandments and added others, above all teaching that we are to "love each other" (John 15:12).

It is God's will that we be holy (1 Thess. 4:3).

It is God's will that we should pray (1 Thess. 5:17).

Romans 12:2 says, "Do not conform any longer to the pattern of this world, but be transformed by the renewing of your mind. Then you will be able to test and approve what God's will is—his good, pleasing and perfect will." If we seek guidance—and we should—it is in texts such as these that the guidance will be found.

Sufficient for Social Reformation

The final area in which we need to know that God's Word is sufficient is the area of social renewal and reform. We live in a declining culture and want to see the lordship of Jesus acknowledged,
justice done, and virtue increase. We want to see the poor relieved
of want and suffering. How can this happen? Not by more government programs or by increased emphasis on social work—though
such things may have a supplementary or stop-gap place—but by
the teaching and practice of the Word of God.

Here is a particularly striking example. In 1535 the Council of
Two Hundred, which governed the city of Geneva, Switzerland,
decided to break with Catholicism and align the city with the
Protestant Reformation. They had very little idea what that meant.
Up to this point the city had been notorious for its riots, gambling,
indecent dancing, drunkenness, adultery, and other vices. The cit-
izens of Geneva would literally run around the streets naked,
singing indecent songs and blaspheming God. They expected this
state of affairs to continue even after they had become Protestants,
and the Council did not know what to do. It had passed regulation
after regulation designed to restrain vice and to remedy the situation. They thought becoming Protestant would solve the problem.
But that did not do any good either. Genuine moral change never
comes from the top down by law, but from the bottom up through
a transformed people. Geneva's morals continued to decline.

But the Council did one thing right. They invited John Calvin
to become Geneva's chief pastor and preacher. He arrived in August
of 1536, a year after the change. He was ignored at first, even by
the Council. He was not even paid the first year. Besides, his first
preaching proved so unpopular that he was dismissed in early 1538
and went to Strasbourg, where he was very happy. He had no desire
to go back to Geneva. Yet, when the situation in Geneva continued
to deteriorate, public opinion turned to him again and, driven by
a sense of duty, Calvin returned. It was September 13, 1541.

Calvin had no weapon but the Bible. From the very first, his
emphasis had been on Bible teaching, and he returned to it now,
picking up precisely where he had left off three and a half years ear-

lier. Calvin preached from the Bible every day, and under the power of that preaching the city began to be transformed. As the people of Geneva acquired knowledge of God's Word and were changed by it, the city became, as John Knox called it later, a New Jerusalem from which the gospel spread to the rest of Europe, England, and the New World. This change made other changes possible. One historian wrote:

> Cleanliness was practically unknown in towns of his generation and epidemics were common and numerous. He moved the Council to make permanent regulations for establishing sanitary conditions and supervision of markets. Beggars were prohibited from the streets, but a hospital and poorhouse were provided and well conducted. Calvin labored zealously for the education of all classes and established the famous Academy, whose influence reached all parts of Europe and even to the British Isles. He urged the council to introduce the cloth and silk industry and thus laid the foundation for the temporal wealth of Geneva. This industry . . . proved especially successful in Geneva because Calvin, through the gospel, created within the individual the love of work, honesty, thrift and cooperation. He taught that capital was not an evil thing, but the blessed result of honest labor and that it could be used for the welfare of mankind. Countries under the influence of Calvinism were invariably connected with growing industry and wealth. . . . It is no mere coincidence that religious and political liberty arose in those countries where Calvinism had penetrated most deeply.[11]

There probably has never been a clearer example of extensive moral and social reform than the transformation of Geneva under the ministry of John Calvin, and it was accomplished almost entirely by the preaching of God's Word.

Think again about 2 Timothy 3. Paul encouraged Timothy to continue on the path of ministry he had been walking because "from infancy you have known the holy Scriptures, which are able to make you wise for salvation through faith in Christ Jesus" (v. 15). Why is the Bible able to do that? It is able to do that because it is "God-breathed" (v. 16). That is, it is the very Word of God and therefore carries within it the authority and very power of God. Yes, and it is useful too. It is useful for "teaching, rebuking, correcting and training in righteousness, so that the man of God may be thoroughly equipped for every good work" (vv. 16-17).

That is exactly it. That is what we need. It is what everybody needs. And only the Word of God is sufficient for it.

F O U R

Christic Alone

Christ Alone

To him who loved us long ago,
Before we came to be,
Who left his throne for earth below
To save a wretch like me:
All praise to Christ from grateful men
Forevermore. Amen.

In 1897, the year of the magnificent jubilee celebration in honor of Queen Victoria, when England was at the height of her colonial power and the rulers of the empire had returned to London in their tall ships for a long summer of self-congratulating days, Rudyard Kipling, the best known and most popular of the British poets, was asked to write a verse for the occasion. He wrote a powerful poem, beginning:

> God of our fathers, known of old,
>   Lord of our far-flung battle line,
> Beneath whose awful Hand we hold
>   Dominion over palm and pine—
> Lord God of Hosts, be with us yet,
>   Lest we forget—lest we forget!

Kipling's "Recessional 1897" was not appreciated. The opinion at the time was that Kipling was passed over as the nation's poet laureate because he had dared to remind his countrymen that earthly success comes from God alone and that God must not be forgotten or fail to be devoutly thanked. No one wanted to think like that in 1897. But Kipling was right, and we must heed that warning ourselves, lest we forget the gospel of salvation by grace alone that is our heritage.

Justification because of Christ alone (*solus Christus*) means that Jesus has done the necessary work of salvation utterly and completely, so that no merit on the part of man, no merit of the saints, no works of ours performed either here or later in purgatory, can add to his completed work. In fact, any attempt to add to Christ's work is a perversion of the gospel and indeed is no gospel at all (Gal. 1:6-9). To proclaim Christ alone is to proclaim him as the Christian's one and only sufficient Prophet, Priest, and King. We need no other prophets to reveal God's word or will. We need no other priests to mediate God's salvation and blessing. We need no other kings to control the thinking and lives of believers. Jesus is everything to us and for us in the gospel.

Yet we are in danger of forgetting that today, because of our idolatrous preoccupation with ourselves. The polls tell us that seventy-six percent of evangelicals believe that man is basically good by nature, and that eighty-six percent believe that the gospel is mostly about God helping us to help ourselves.

The Cambridge Declaration protests:

> As evangelical faith has become secularized, its interests have been blurred with those of the culture. The result is a loss of absolute values, permissive individualism, and a substitution of wholeness for holiness, recovery for repentance, intuition for truth, feeling for belief, chance for providence, and immediate gratification for enduring hope. Christ and his cross have moved from the center of our vision.[1]

How can it be that "Christ and his cross have moved from the center of our vision"?

If there is anything that does rightly characterize the evangelical churches in our time, it is an emphasis upon Jesus. Yes, but it is often only a Jesus who panders to our selfish desires and felt needs. The "gospel" of our day has a lot to do with self-esteem, good mental attitudes, and worldly success. There is almost no preaching about sin, hell, judgment, or the wrath of God, even less about doctrines that center in the Lord of glory and his Cross: grace, redemption, atonement, propitiation, justification, and even faith. Moreover, lacking a biblical and well-understood theology, evangelicals have fallen prey to the consumerism of our times. A therapeutic worldview has replaced the classical Christian categories I have mentioned—sin, grace, redemption, and others—and many have identified the gospel with such modern idols as a particular political philosophy, psychology, or sociology.

To the extent that Christ and his Cross are no longer central, modern evangelicalism has become a movement shaped only by popular whim and sentimentality.

THE CROSS AT THE CENTER

It is impossible to overestimate the importance of Christ's Cross. For whether we are thinking about the necessity of the Cross, the meaning of the Cross, the preaching of the Cross, the offense of the Cross, or the way of the Cross—however we may think about it— in every case what we are saying, and must be saying, is that the Cross is central to Christianity. Indeed, we are saying more. We are saying that without the Cross of Jesus Christ there is no true Christianity at all.

Emil Brunner wrote a book on Christ's person and work called *The Mediator,* in which he linked a right understanding of the Cross to the Reformation. He said, "Luther certainly hit the nail on the head when he described Christian theology . . . as a *theologia crucis* [a theology of the Cross]." Indeed, Brunner added, "The whole struggle of the Reformation for the *sola fide,* the *soli deo gloria,* was simply the struggle for the right interpretation of the Cross. He who understands the Cross aright—this is the opinion of the Reformers—understands the Bible, he understands Jesus Christ." He then quotes Luther directly: "'Therefore this text—"He bore our sins"—must be understood particularly thoroughly as the foundation upon which stands the whole of the New Testament or the Gospel, as that which alone distinguishes us and our religion from all other religions. . . . Whoever believes this article of faith is secure against all errors, and God the Holy Ghost is necessarily with him.'"[2]

If that is true, if the Cross of Christ is the very heart and essence of Christianity, we should expect, on one hand, that the theology of the Cross would be simplicity itself: "Christ died for our sins according to the Scriptures" (1 Cor. 15:3), and "Believe in the Lord Jesus, and you will be saved" (Acts 16:31). It must be accessible to the understanding and belief of everyone. And so it is! The Cross is presented in precisely that way in the Bible—simply and with the most direct demand for one's faith.

On the other hand, if the Cross is the very essence of Christianity, we may expect it to stretch our minds to the utmost. Indeed, we may expect that in some measure the full meaning of the Cross will always lie greatly beyond our grasp, beyond any exhaustive comprehension on our parts. In this double sense, the theology of the Cross might be described by the words one writer used to describe the theology of the fourth Gospel. He called it "a pool in which a child can wade" as well as "an ocean in which an elephant can swim."

We begin to see the complexity of the Cross as soon as we list the words commonly used to explain it: substitution, sacrifice, satisfaction, atonement, expiation, propitiation, purchase, redemption, ransom, mediation, reconciliation, and so on.

Or when we begin to list important texts. These texts are found throughout the Bible, in the Old Testament as well as in the New Testament. We remember that when Jesus began to explain the meaning of his death to the two disciples who were making their way home to Emmaus after the Resurrection, he did so from the whole Old Testament. We are told, "And beginning with Moses and all the Prophets, he explained to them what was said in all the Scriptures concerning himself" (Luke 24:27). That refers to what Jews call the *tenach*. The word *tenach* is composed of three consonants, each standing for one of the three major parts of the Old Testament: "T" for the *torah* or law of Moses; "N" for *neviim* or prophets; and "K" for *ketuvim*, that is, the writings or the Scriptures. Jesus was teaching that the meaning of his death is to be found throughout the Old Testament, from Genesis to Malachi.

And that is what we discover. In Genesis, we read of the offspring of the woman who will "crush" the serpent's head while Satan strikes "his heel" (Gen. 3:15). That is the first announcement of the gospel. It refers to the Cross. Later we read of God's promise of a son to Abraham, one through whom "all nations of the earth will be blessed" (Gen. 12:3; 17:15-16; 22:18). Ultimately the son who was to be born in Abraham's line of descent was Jesus.

Isaiah writes of one who was

> . . . pierced for our transgressions,
>   [and] . . . crushed for our iniquities;
> the punishment that brought us peace was upon him,
>   and by his wounds we are healed.
> We all, like sheep, have gone astray,
>   each of us has turned to his own way;
> and the LORD has laid on him
>   the iniquity of us all (Isa. 53:5-6).

In the Law, particularly in Leviticus, the Cross was prefigured in the instructions for how the sacrifices were to be offered and by the details for the construction and use of the ark of the covenant that stood within the Most Holy Place of the wilderness tabernacle and later the Jerusalem temple. Psalm 22 provides a particularly graphic prediction of Christ's death by crucifixion. Zechariah speaks of a future generation that will look on "the one they have pierced" and mourn for him (Zech. 12:10). Malachi, at the end of the Old Testament, writes of a "sun of righteousness" that "will rise with healing in its wings" (Mal. 4:2).

There are even more texts about the Cross in the New Testament, which is what we would expect:

"You are to give him the name Jesus, because he will save his people from their sins" (Matt. 1:21).

"This is my body given for you. . . . This cup is the new covenant in my blood, which is poured out for you" (Luke 22:19, 20).

"Look, the Lamb of God, who takes away the sin of the world!" (John 1:29).

God made him who had no sin to be sin for us, so that in him we might become the righteousness of God (2 Cor. 5:21).

Just as man is destined to die once, and after that to face judgment, so Christ was sacrificed once to take away the sins of many people (Heb. 9:27-28).

He himself bore our sins in his body on the tree, so that we might die to sins and live for righteousness; by his wounds you have been healed (1 Pet. 2:24).

For Christ died for sins once for all, the righteous for the unrighteous, to bring you to God (1 Pet. 3:18).

To him who loves us and has freed us from our sins by his blood, and has made us to be a kingdom and priests to serve his God and Father—to him be glory and power for ever and ever! Amen (Rev. 1:5-6).

Those texts introduce us to such ideas as: a ransom; taking away or bearing sin; a blood covenant; sacrifice; redemption; and a purchase with blood.

How do we go about handling a topic both as simple and also as rich and complex as the Cross of Christ? One way we can do so is by looking at the three most important words for grasping what the Cross is about and then bringing in a number of verses that relate to those three themes. The words most essential for understanding what the Cross is about are *satisfaction, sacrifice,* and *substitution*. They are easy to remember because each begins with the letter *s*.

THE CROSS AS SATISFACTION

I start with *satisfaction* because satisfaction has to do with the character of God which we have offended. It has to do with sin. To make satisfaction means to make reparation for damage done, to make amends, or to provide compensation. In this case the damage is to God's law and honor. We cannot understand the Cross until we take God's honor seriously.

Anselm of Canterbury was an Italian who had settled in France but was appointed archbishop of England in 1093, twenty-seven years after the Norman Conquest. His greatest contribution to theology was to the doctrine of the Atonement in a work titled *Cur Deus Homo?* which means "Why the God-Man?" or, to put it in more colloquial language, "Why Did God Become Man?" The book explains the Incarnation by the Cross, arguing that God became man to make an atonement for sin as the only possible ground for our salvation.

Anselm began with a definition of sin, which he explained as an infinite offense by man against God's honor. It is "not to render his due to God" (i, xi). Being an inexcusable disobedience of God's known will, sin insults him. "Nothing is less tolerable in the order of things, than for the creature to take away the honor due to the Creator and not repay what he takes away" (i, xiii). God must act justly, and "if it is not fitting for God to do anything unjustly or without due order, it does not belong to his freedom or kindness or will to forgive unpunished the sinner who does not repay to God what he took away" (i, xii); "God maintains nothing more justly than the honor of his dignity" (i, xiii), Anselm wrote.[3]

Later writers have called attention to the dangers in such language—to imagine a standard outside of God that must be satisfied or to restrict the meaning of the Cross to a simple debt transaction. But Anselm was not as simplistic as this. He knew that the standard that needed to be satisfied is God's own character, what he is in himself but has expressed outwardly in his law. He also knew that language about paying a debt is only metaphorical. What is important is that Anselm at the beginning of his work was calling attention to an utterly indispensable point—that in order to understand the Cross we must begin by considering the seriousness of sin. If we do not understand the seriousness of sin, we will assume that all God needs to do is forgive us, indeed, that he owes us forgiveness. "We forgive other people," we think. "Why shouldn't God just forgive us?"

This is what lay behind the well-known words of the French philosopher Voltaire, who expressed the superficial view of God held by most moderns when he quipped, *"Dieu pardonnera, c'est son metier!"* ("God will pardon; that's his business!"). But God cannot "just pardon," and to think so is itself an offense. Emil Brunner had it right when he said of Voltaire's remark that there has never been a "more impious saying." Why? Because "there are no human conditions in which we have the right to expect that God will forgive us as a matter of course."[4] Anselm said that if anyone imagines that God can simply forgive us, that person has "not yet considered what a heavy weight sin is" (*nondum considerasti quanti ponderis sit peccatum,* i, xxi).[5]

What can be done? Obviously God must save us. We cannot achieve salvation for ourselves, because we are the ones who have gotten into trouble in the first place. We have done so by our rebellion against God's decrees. Moreover, we have suffered from the effects of sin to such a degree that even our will is bound; therefore we cannot even *want* to please God, let alone actually please him. On the other hand, said Anselm—apparently contradicting himself on this first point—salvation must be achieved by man, for man is the one who has wronged God and who therefore must make the wrong right. Given this situation, salvation can only be achieved by one who is both God and man, that is, by Jesus Christ:

> It would not have been right for the restoration of human nature to be left undone, and . . . it could not have been done unless man paid what was owing to God for sin. But the debt

was so great that, while man alone owed it, only God could pay it, so that the same person must be both man and God. Thus it was necessary for God to take manhood into the unity of his person, so that he who in his own nature ought to pay and could not should be in a person who could. . . . The life of this man was so sublime, so precious, that it can suffice to pay what is owing for the sins of the whole world, and infinitely more.[6]

Anselm's doctrine must not to be misunderstood, as many theologians have misunderstood it, in some cases willfully. If we would keep the matter of satisfaction straight in our minds, we must remember that it is God who initiates and carries out this action. If we forget that, we may find ourselves thinking of God as somehow remote from the Atonement and thus only requiring it of some poor victim as an arbitrary price paid to satisfy his wounded honor or an abstract concept of justice. God is not rigid, harsh, and cruel. On the contrary, it is out of God's immense but inexplicable love that he designed and then carried out the Atonement. Nevertheless, the doctrine of a satisfaction made by God the Son to God the Father on behalf of sinners is the essential starting point for grasping the meaning of the Cross, because it is only the concept of satisfaction that takes sin seriously. Sin is an infinite offense against God's utterly upright character, and any adequate plan of salvation must satisfy God first of all.

The best theologians have always seen this.

Martin Luther expressed it when he wrote, "Since all of us, born in sin and God's enemies, have earned nothing but eternal wrath and hell so that everything we are and can do is damned, and there is no help or way of getting out of this predicament . . . therefore another man had to step into our place, namely Jesus Christ, God and man, and had to render satisfaction and make payment for sin through his suffering and death."[7]

This is the essential meaning of such texts as:

"Even the Son of Man did not come to be served, but to serve, and to give his life as a ransom for many" (Mark 10:45).

> Christ redeemed us from the curse of the law by becoming a curse for us (Gal. 3:13).

> For you know that it was not with perishable things such as silver or gold that you were redeemed from the empty way of life handed down to you from your forefathers, but with the precious blood of Christ, a lamb without blemish or defect (1 Pet. 1:18-19).

> "You are worthy to take the scroll and to open its seals, because you were slain, and with your blood you purchased men for God from every tribe and language and people and nation. You have made them to be a kingdom and priests to serve our God, and they will reign on the earth" (Rev. 5:9-10).

Each of these verses speaks of paying a necessary price, satisfying a proper requirement, or making a purchase. Thus, each has to do with providing satisfaction to God for the debt we owe him.

THE CROSS AS SACRIFICE

The second important word for understanding the meaning of the Cross is *sacrifice.* Sacrifice has to do with satisfying God's wrath. This balances any tendency we might have to think of the achievement of the Cross abstractly, which we might do if we were to think in terms of satisfaction only. A debt may be impersonal, but wrath is not. Wrath is a personal matter. It means that God is personally offended. He is angry, and his wrath must be turned aside if we are to be reconciled to him.

This is what is meant by *propitiation,* a word the New International Version renders "a sacrifice of atonement" or simply "atonement." It occurs in Romans 3:25 ("God presented him as *a sacrifice of atonement,* through faith in his blood"); Hebrews 2:17 ("He had to be made like his brothers in every way, in order that he might become a merciful and faithful high priest in service to God, and that he might make *atonement* for the sins of the people"); 1 John 2:2 ("He is the *atoning sacrifice* for our sins"); and 1 John 4:10

("This is love: not that we loved God, but that he loved us and sent his Son as *an atoning sacrifice* for our sins").

In ancient pagan religion, propitiation referred to what a worshiper did when he or she presented a sacrifice to one of the gods or goddesses. It was an act by which the wrath of the offended god could be appeased or turned aside.

There have been vigorous objections to this understanding of the Cross in our day, above all because it presupposes God's wrath and therefore the necessity of turning God's holy, justified wrath aside. Propitiation and sacrifice both teach that God's wrath must be dealt with. But modern thinkers regard wrath as an inappropriate concept for Christianity. "We can understand how the idea of propitiation might be appropriate in an ancient, pagan society where God was thought to be vacillating, capricious, and often angry," such persons might say. "But this is not the God of Christianity. God is not angry. He does not need to be appeased. God has shown us that he is a God of love. All we need to do is recognize his love and receive his forgiveness."

One theologian states sharply:

> [Those who hold to] the 'fire and brimstone' school of theology, who revel in ideas such as that Christ was made a sacrifice to appease an angry God, or that the cross was a legal transaction in which an innocent victim was made to pay the penalty for the crimes of others, a propitiation of a stern God, find no support in Paul. These notions came into Christian theology by way of the legalistic minds of the medieval churchmen; they are not biblical Christianity.[8]

How extraordinary!

I grant that Anselm was a medieval scholastic. I have warned against some wrong deductions from his writings. But how can any informed person say that the anger and wrath of God are not biblical ideas? Far from being absent from the Bible or even being minimized by it, the Bible actually teaches—from Genesis to Revelation—that it is precisely the wrath of God that is our problem. In Genesis God destroys the earth by the Flood. In Revelation

he displays his wrath in his many final judgments. We are subject
to God's wrath now because of sin. So if the wrath of God cannot
be turned aside by someone or in some way, we will perish. It is precisely propitiation that we should be looking for. John Murray
wrote, "Instead of stumbling at this concept we should rather
anticipate that the precise category suited to the need and liability
created by the wrath of God would be enlisted to describe or define
the provision of God's grace."[9]

Here are two important points to remember:

1. *Although God's wrath is not like the capricious anger of the
pagan deities, his wrath is nevertheless a true wrath against sin; and
it is this true and proper wrath that must be dealt with.*

We may feel, because of our particular cultural prejudices, that
the wrath of God and the love of God are incompatible. But the
Bible teaches that God is both wrath and love at the same time.
What is more, his wrath is not just a small and insignificant element alongside his far more significant and overwhelming love.
God's wrath is a strong character element. God loathes sin and must
punish it.

2. *Although propitiation means turning God's wrath aside, in the
Bible this is never a case of human beings appeasing God's wrath but
rather of God himself satisfying his wrath through the death of his own
Son, Jesus Christ.*

In pagan rituals, sacrifices were made by people trying to placate God, to make for themselves an atonement for their sin. In the
Bible it is never *we* who take the initiative or make the sacrifice; it
is God himself who, out of his great love for sinners, provides the
way by which his wrath against sin may be averted. Moreover, he
is himself that way—in Jesus. God himself placates his own wrath
against sin so that his love may go out to save sinners. John Stott
observes, "This was already clear in the Old Testament, in which
the sacrifices were recognized not as human works but as divine
gifts. They did not make God gracious; they were provided by a gracious God in order that he might act graciously towards his sinful
people. 'I have given it to you,' God said of the sacrificial blood, 'to
make atonement for yourselves on the altar' (Lev. 17:11)."[10]

This brings us to one of the most beautiful pictures of the work of Christ in all the Bible: the ark of the covenant, which was kept within the Most Holy Place of the Jewish wilderness tabernacle and was the focal point of Israel's worship.

The ark was a wooden box about a yard long, covered with gold, and made to contain the stone tables of the law that Moses had received on Mount Sinai. (The first set of tables had been broken, but a new set had been written.) This box had a cover called the mercy seat, and upon the mercy seat, at each end, facing each other, were statues of cherubim (angels) whose wings stretched upward and then outward, almost meeting directly over the ark. In a symbolic way, God was imagined to dwell above the ark, between or over the outstretched wings of the cherubim.

As it stands, the ark is a picture of judgment, intended to produce dread in the worshiper through a disclosure of his or her sin. For what does God see as he looks down upon earth from between the outstretched wings of the cherubim? Clearly, he sees the law of Moses which each of us has broken. He sees that he must act toward us in judgment. God cannot ignore sin; sin must be punished.

But this is where the mercy seat comes in, and this is why it is called the *mercy* seat. Once a year, on the Day of Atonement, the Jewish high priest entered the Most Holy Place to make propitiation for the people's sins. Propitiation is the very word which (in Greek) was used to translate "mercy seat." Moments before, the high priest had offered (in the outer courtyard of the tabernacle) a sacrifice for his own sin and the sins of his family. Now he took the blood of a second animal, entered the Most Holy Place, and carefully sprinkled the blood of that sacrifice upon the mercy seat, which was the ark's covering. What is symbolized now? Now, as God looks down from between the outstretched wings of the cherubim, he sees not the law of Moses which we have broken but the blood of the innocent victim. He sees that punishment has been meted out. Propitiation has been made, and his love goes out to save all who come to him through faith in that sacrifice.

Jesus told a parable about two men who went to the temple to pray. One was a Pharisee; the other was a tax collector. The Pharisee stood up to pray—as everyone would have agreed he should do: "Come here, Mr. Pharisee. Stand up where we can all hear you. Be quiet, everyone. The Pharisee is going to pray."

And pray he did. He prayed a magnificent prayer—about himself: "God, I thank you that I am not like other men—robbers, evildoers, adulterers—or even like this tax collector. I fast twice a week and give a tenth of all I get" (Luke 18:11-12). The Pharisee was not lying. He really did give a tenth of his income to the temple. He really did fast twice a week. He was not a thief or an adulterer. Moreover, I am sure others would have concurred in this evaluation. Here was an outstanding man, a credit to his community. The point of Jesus' parable depends on recognizing that if anyone could hope to be accepted by God on the basis of his character or good works, it was this Pharisee.

Then there was the tax collector. He "stood at a distance"—where he belonged. Jesus said of him, "He would not even look up to heaven, but beat his breast and said, 'God, have mercy on me, a sinner'" (v. 13). And why not? He *was* a sinner. He had plenty to beat his breast about.

It is hard to imagine a greater contrast than the one between these two men: moral versus immoral; noble versus base; proud versus shameful; self-confident versus cringing. Yet when the Lord ended his story, he reversed the judgment every one of his hearers had been making and declared: "I tell you that this man [the tax collector], rather than the other, went home justified before God. For everyone who exalts himself will be humbled, and he who humbles himself will be exalted" (v. 14). No cinematic melodrama or dime-store novel ever had a more surprising ending than this parable.

Why did the tax collector, rather than the Pharisee, go home justified? It is true that the Pharisee was a sinner. He was a sinner in spite of his self-righteousness. But so was the tax collector. The only differences between the two men were that the tax collector knew he was a sinner, while the Pharisee did not know it; and the tax collector approached God, not on the basis of his good works (which he did not have), but on the basis of God's provision, symbolized by the mercy seat and the propitiation that took place there. The tax collector's prayer literally reads, "God, be 'mercy-seated' to me, the sinner."

The prayer is worth exploring. The first word of the prayer is "God"; the last word is "sinner." This reflects what happens when a human being becomes aware of the true God. When a person becomes conscious of God, he does not proceed unchanged in his supposed "righteousness," as the Pharisee did. Rather he becomes conscious of sin, and the more so the closer to God he comes. We know that the tax collector knew God because he knew he was— and did not hesitate to describe himself as—a sinner.

Then, between the beginning of the prayer ("God") and the end of it ("me, a sinner") are the words "be mercy-seated to me." This shows that the tax collector also understood propitiation. He knew that between the presence of the Holy God (who looked down in judgment upon the law which he had broken) and himself there had to come the blood of the sacrificial victim. He was coming to God on the basis of the mercy already provided by God through the sacrifice. The tax collector was saying, "Treat me on the basis of the blood sprinkled upon the mercy seat." No one can be saved without propitiation.

THE CROSS AS SUBSTITUTION

We need to add one more concept to our understanding of the Cross of Christ. We have looked at satisfaction and sacrifice. Now we must think about *substitution*. The idea here is that we need a mediator, a word Paul uses in 1 Timothy 2:5 and the author of Hebrews uses in Hebrews 8:6; 9:15; and 12:24. A mediator is one who comes between two parties in order to represent each to the other or to reconcile them. This is precisely what we need. We need a person who can come between God and ourselves and accomplish what we cannot accomplish. We can never satisfy justice or turn wrath aside ourselves. But Jesus could and did.

It is Jesus' mediatorial work that makes our justification possible. Jesus bore the punishment for our sin in our place, and it is because of this sin-bearing atonement that God is able to impute Christ's righteousness to us, which is how we are justified. Referring to justification as "the most incomprehensible thing that exists," Emil Brunner wrote, "Justification means this miracle: that Christ takes our place and we take his."[11] The ancient church father Irenaeus expressed it in nearly similar language when he said, "For the sake of his infinite love he [Jesus] has become what we are in order that he may make us entirely what he is."[12]

Is anything more important than this?

Once when the Swiss theologian Karl Barth was asked what he thought was the most important word in the New Testament, he answered, *"Huper." Huper* is a preposition meaning "on behalf of" or "in place of." So when Barth called *huper* the most important word, he meant that the most important of all truths is that in salvation Jesus takes our place to bear the punishment for our sins so that "in him we might become the righteousness of God" (2 Cor. 5:21).

It is not uncommon for Jesus' saving work to be reduced by well-meaning teachers merely to his death on the Cross. True, the suffering of Jesus for our sin *is* the center of the gospel message. There could have been no salvation for us unless Jesus had died for us, bearing the penalty due for our transgressions. This doctrine is of fundamental importance. Yet it is only one-half of what is necessary. It is the negative side. The positive side is the imputation of Christ's righteousness to us, so that we are now able to stand before God clothed in that righteousness; for that to happen, Jesus needed to live a life of perfect righteousness. In other words, his perfect, active obedience was necessary for our salvation.

This two-fold aspect of salvation is made clear by Paul in Romans 4. In chapter 3 he has explained the way of salvation through the work of Jesus Christ, who by his death turned aside God's wrath against us for our sin. This was how God was able to justify or declare the sinner to be righteous, while himself remaining just. Since Paul speaks of a "righteousness from God" and also an atoning work of Christ, both the negative and positive sides of this saving transaction are affirmed. Yet this becomes particularly clear in chapter 4.

In that chapter Paul is proving his doctrine from the Old Testament, and to do so he brings forward two examples of people who were saved: Abraham, the greatest of the patriarchs; and David, the greatest of the kings. In the case of Abraham, Paul cites Genesis 15:6, writing, "What does the Scripture say? 'Abraham believed God, and it was credited to him as righteousness'" (Rom. 4:3). That is the positive side, the imputation of Christ's righteousness to us. In the case of David, Paul cites Psalm 32:1-2:

> Blessed are they whose transgressions are forgiven,
>   whose sins are covered.
> Blessed is the man
>   whose sin the Lord will never count against him
> (Rom. 4:7-8).

That is the negative side, the imputation of our sin to Christ, who died for our sin.

Not surprisingly, hymn writers have expressed both sides of this amazing exchange. Horatio G. Spafford celebrated the first half of the transaction when he wrote:

> My sin—O the bliss of this glorious thought!—
>   My sin, not in part, but the whole,
> Is nailed to the cross, and I bear it no more:
>   Praise the Lord!
>   Praise the Lord! O my soul.[13]

Count Zinzendorf was thinking of the second half when he wrote:

> Jesus, thy blood and righteousness
> My beauty are, my glorious dress;
> 'Midst flaming worlds, in these arrayed,
> With joy shall I lift up my head.[14]

It is because of this two-fold transaction that we, who are sinners, are able to stand forgiven and clothed with righteousness before the holy God.

Here is H. E. Guillebaud's summary of all three of these important, nonnegotiable truths: satisfaction, sacrifice, and substitution.

> God is not only perfectly holy, but the source and pattern of
> holiness. He is the origin and the upholder of the moral order
> of the universe. He *must* be just. The Judge of all the earth
> *must* do right. Therefore it was impossible by the necessities
> of his own being that he should deal lightly with sin, and
> compromise the claims of holiness. If sin could be forgiven at
> all, it must be on some basis which would vindicate the holy
> law of God, which is not a mere code, but the moral order of
> the whole creation. But such vindication must be supremely
> costly. Costly to whom? Not to the forgiven sinner, for there
> could be no price asked from him for his forgiveness; both
> because the cost is far beyond his reach, and because God
> loves to give and not to sell. Therefore, God himself under-
> took to pay a cost, to offer a sacrifice, so tremendous that the
> gravity of his condemnation of sin should be absolutely
> beyond question even as he forgave it, while at the same time
> the love which impelled him to pay the price would be the
> wonder of the angels, and would call forth the worshiping
> gratitude of the redeemed sinner.
>
> On Calvary this price was paid, paid by *God*: the Son giv-
> ing himself, bearing our sin and its curse; the Father giving
> the Son, his only Son whom he loved. But it was paid by God
> become man, who not only took the place of guilty man, but
> also was his representative. . . .
>
> He offered himself as a sacrifice in our stead, bearing our
> sin in his own body on the tree. He suffered, not only awful
> physical anguish, but also the unthinkable spiritual horror of
> becoming identified with the sin to which he was infinitely
> opposed. He thereby came under the curse of sin, so that for
> a time even his perfect fellowship with his Father was broken.
> Thus God proclaimed his infinite abhorrence of sin by being
> willing himself to suffer all that, in place of the guilty ones, in
> order that he might justly forgive. Thus the love of God found
> its perfect fulfillment, because he did not hold back from even
> that uttermost sacrifice, in order that we might be saved from
> eternal death through what he endured.[15]

A number of conclusions follow from these teachings.

1. *According to the Bible, Calvary and not Bethlehem is the center of Christianity.* It has been a popular idea in some theological circles that the Incarnation is the important truth of Christianity, that is, God identifying himself with man, and that the Atonement is something like an afterthought. But according to biblical teaching, the reason for the Incarnation is that a God-man was required to die for our salvation. Therefore, as J. I. Packer has written, "The crucial significance of the cradle at Bethlehem lies in its place in the sequence of steps down that led the Son of God to the cross of Calvary, and we do not understand it until we see it in that context."[16] To focus on the birth of Jesus apart from the Cross leads to false sentimentality and neglect of the horror and magnitude of sin.

2. *If the death of Christ on the Cross is the true focal point of Christianity, then there can be no gospel without the Cross.* Christmas by itself is no gospel. The life of Christ is no gospel. Even the Resurrection by itself is no gospel. The Good News is not just that God became man, nor that God has spoken in Christ to reveal a proper way of life for us, nor even that death, our great enemy, has been conquered. The Good News is that sin has been dealt with, that Jesus suffered its penalty for us as our representative, and that all who believe in him can look forward confidently to heaven.

Any "gospel" that talks merely about the Christ-event, meaning the Incarnation without the Atonement, is a false gospel. Any gospel that talks about the love of God without showing that love led him to pay the ultimate price for sin in the person of his Son on the Cross, is a false gospel. The only true gospel is the gospel of the "one mediator" who gave himself for us (1 Tim. 2:5, 6). If our churches are not preaching this gospel, they are not preaching the gospel at all, and if they are not preaching the gospel, they are not true churches. Evangelicalism desperately needs to rediscover its roots and recover its essential biblical bearing at this point.

3. *Finally, just as there can be no gospel without the Atonement, so also there can be no Christian life without it.* Without the Atonement, religion, even the Christian religion, becomes a type of human self-deification and leads to brazen arrogance and pre-

sumption, which is what much of evangelicalism has become and is doing. With the Atonement, the achievement of the Cross draws forth love from us and becomes an example of the kind of self-sacrifice we should be making. We are led to give all we have to Jesus Christ, because Jesus gave all he had for us. In 1701, Isaac Watts wrote:

> Were the whole realm of nature mine,
> That were a present far too small;
> Love so amazing, so divine,
> Demands my soul, my life, my all.[17]

Watts was right. The love of Christ, displayed in his death on the Cross, really does demand our all.

Grace Alone

All creation joins in praising
Christ, the Savior of our race,
Drawn from ev'ry tribe and nation,
People, language, time and place:
"Holy, holy, holy, holy
Is our God, the God of grace."

Evangelicals do not deny grace any more than the church of the Middle Ages denied this essential Bible doctrine. Evangelicals do not want to be heretics. The problem is that, although we affirm the grace of God in theory, we reject it by neglect. We do not seem to think it is important.

When the Reformers spoke about "grace alone" (*sola gratia*), they were saying that sinners have no claim upon God, none at all; that God owes them nothing but punishment for their sins; and that, if he saves them in spite of their sins, which he does in the case of those who are being saved, it is only because it pleases him to do it and for no other reason. Today, large numbers of evangelicals undermine and effectively destroy this doctrine by supposing that human beings are basically good; that God owes everyone a chance to be saved; and that, if we are saved, in the final analysis it is because of our own good decision to receive the Jesus who is offered to us.

This is why the doctrine of election is opposed by so many. It doesn't seem fair to them. But as soon as we introduce the doctrine of fairness, we introduce a standard of right by which God has to save all or at least give everyone an equal chance of being saved. And that is not grace! If God were motivated only by what is right, without any consideration of a grace made possible by the work of Christ, all would be condemned and all would spend eternity in hell. This is because "there is no one righteous, not even one; there is no one who understands, no one who seeks God" (Rom. 3:10-11).

Here is the way the Alliance of Confessing Evangelicals explained the problem in the Cambridge Declaration, the paper prepared by pastors and church leaders in 1996:

> Unwarranted confidence in human ability is a product of fallen human nature. This false confidence now fills the evangelical world—from the self-esteem gospel to the health and wealth gospel, from those who have transformed the gospel into a product to be sold and sinners into consumers who want to buy, to others who treat Christian faith as being true simply because it works. This silences the doctrine of justification regardless of the official commitments of our churches.
>
> God's grace in Christ is not merely necessary but is the sole efficient cause of salvation. We confess that human beings are born spiritually dead and are incapable even of cooperating with regenerating grace.

The Declaration adds these solemn affirmations and denials:

> We reaffirm that in salvation we are rescued from God's wrath by his grace alone. It is the supernatural work of the Holy Spirit that brings us to Christ by releasing us from our bondage to sin and raising us from spiritual death to spiritual life.
>
> We deny that salvation is in any sense a human work. Human methods, techniques or strategies by themselves cannot accomplish this transformation. Faith is not produced by our unregenerated human nature.[1]

Today's evangelical church needs to recapture those strong convictions about grace. For if it does not, it is not just failing to get its theology right, it is failing to be a true church. It is denying the gospel.

AMAZING GRACE OR BORING GRACE?

Here is a trivia question you can ask your friends at your next dinner party: Of all the songs ever written, which song has been recorded the greatest number of times by the greatest number of different vocal artists? The answer, as you might expect from the subject matter of this chapter, is "Amazing Grace," the classic Christian hymn written in 1779 by the slave trader turned preacher, John Newton:

> Amazing grace! how sweet the sound
> That saved a wretch like me!
> I once was lost but now am found,
> Was blind, but now I see.

Amazing grace really is amazing. It is the most amazing thing in the universe, more amazing even than neutrons and neutrinos, quarks and quasars, and black holes. But like all familiar things, grace has lost its ability to enthrall most people. Instead, as theologian J. I. Packer has observed, amazing grace has for many people become "boring grace."[2]

How can that be? How can a theme that was a cardinal doctrine of the Protestant Reformation and has thrilled Christian people for centuries be thought boring? If you talk to church people about next year's operating budget, you will find them interested. You can interest them in social programs or building a new addition to the education wing. You can talk to them about the latest baseball scores or Wall Street listings or national politics. But try to discuss the grace of God and you will discover that they are suddenly in a field of discourse quite beyond their capacities. They will not contradict you. They will listen. But they will have nothing to contribute. Often you will be met only with blank stares. What could have caused such indifference, even among churchgoers?

Packer suggests it is a failure to understand and "feel in one's heart" four great truths that the doctrine of grace presupposes: 1) the sinfulness of sin; 2) God's judgment; 3) man's spiritual inability; and 4) God's sovereign freedom.[3]

THE SINFULNESS OF SIN

It is a sad, harmful, and evil characteristic of sin not to recognize how serious it is and to excuse it by treating it lightly. Those who have come to understand the holiness of God and the nature of his grace to sinners in spite of our sin do not do this. Like the remorseful tax collector, they stand in awe of God and cry out for mercy: "God, have mercy on me, a sinner" (Luke 18:13). They do not treat sin as if it were inconsequential.

King David is an Old Testament example. After he had been brought to acknowledge his sin through the words of the prophet Nathan, David wrote an affecting confession of sin which we know as Psalm 51. It begins with a cry for mercy, followed immediately by a vivid acknowledgment of his transgression. In verse 1 David used three words to express the immeasurable wonder of God's grace: "mercy," "unfailing love," and "compassion." In verses 1 and 2 he used three corresponding words to express the sinfulness of his sin.

The first word is "transgression" (Hebrew, *peshah*). This word refers to "crossing a forbidden boundary" with the thought that this is serious "rebellion." You may recall from the annals of Julius Caesar that as long as the general remained to the north of the River Rubicon he was on peaceful terms with the Roman senate. But once he crossed the Rubicon, which the senate had forbidden him to do, he was at war with that legislative body. Caesar did cross, crying, *Alea iacta est* ("The die is cast"), and civil war erupted. That is what we have done with God. We have crossed the boundary of his moral law and consequently are at war with him. "It is not merely, then, that we go against some abstract propriety, or break some impersonal law of nature when we do wrong, but that we rebel against a rightful Sovereign," wrote Alexander Maclaren.[4]

The second word is "iniquity" (Hebrew, *hawon*). This means "perversion" and refers to what we call "original sin" or the innate "depravity" of our natures. Significantly, it is also the word used in the first part of verse 5, where David says he was "sinful" from birth.

The third word is "sin" itself (Hebrew, *chattath*). This means "falling short" or "missing the mark." We miss God's high mark of perfection, falling short of it in the same way an arrow might fall short of a target. But it is also true that sin misses its own mark, since by sinning we never hit what we are aiming at.

These three words occur again later in Psalm 51 (vv. 3, 4, 5, 9, and 13), where it is clear that they refer to David's personal failure: "*my* transgressions," "*my* iniquity" and "*my* sin." The words also occur in verses 1 and 2 of Psalm 32, another psalm of confession, though the New International Version does not use the word "iniquity" to translate *hawon* in that psalm. It uses "sin" to translate both *hawon* and *chattath*. The apostle Paul quotes these verses in Romans 4 as part of his teaching about our sin being imputed to Jesus, so that it might not be counted against us; and his righteousness being imputed to us, so that we might be justified before God:

> Blessed are they
>   whose transgressions are forgiven,
>   whose sins are covered.
> Blessed is the man
>   whose sin the Lord will never count against him
> (Rom. 4:7-8; Ps. 32:1-2).

The nature of sin has left everyone in a deplorable state before God, a state Paul summarizes beginning with verse 9 of chapter 3. According to Paul's summary, Jews are not better than Gentiles, nor are Gentiles better than Jews. Instead all are alike under sin, and all are thus subject to the wrath and final judgment of a holy God. Earlier Paul had explained how the race had fallen deeper and deeper into sin because of its rebellion against God. Now, quoting from Psalms 14:1-3 and 53:1-3 to show that this is God's assessment and not merely his own opinion, Paul writes:

> "There is no one righteous, not even one;
>   there is no one who understands,
>   no one who seeks God" (Rom. 3:10-11).

1. *No one is righteous.* In the first part of his summary the apostle writes of man's moral nature and concludes that the human race is unrighteous. This does not mean merely that we are a bit less righteous than we need to be to somehow get to heaven. It means that from God's point of view human beings have no righteousness at all—none, that is, that will satisfy him. We may be righteous in our own eyes and sometimes even in the eyes of other people, if they do not know us too well. But we do not have any genuine righteousness at all. All our comparisons with other people do is keep us from appreciating or appropriating God's amazing saving grace.

2. *No one understands.* The second pronouncement Paul makes about human beings is that no one understands spiritual things. This refers to a lack of spiritual perception and not merely to a lack of human knowledge. If we think on the human level, comparing the understanding of one person with that of another, we can see that some people have good minds and obviously understand a great deal, and since we are impressed by that we will be misled about their spiritual condition. We need to learn that, as far as spiritual matters are concerned, no one either truly understands or seeks God.

Paul provides his own commentary on the teaching that "no one . . . understands" in the first two chapters of 1 Corinthians. The Corinthians were mostly Greeks. They were proud of their cultural heritage and prized the wisdom of their outstanding philosophers—people like Socrates, Plato, and Aristotle. Paul reminds them, however, that when he was with them he did not try to impress them with his wisdom; rather, he determined to know nothing among them "except Jesus Christ and him crucified" (1 Cor. 2:2), for the power is in that gospel. He explains his decision in two ways.

First, human wisdom has shown itself bankrupt so far as coming to know God is concerned. Paul says:

> The message of the cross is foolishness to those who are perishing, but to us who are being saved it is the power of God. For it is written:
>
>> "I will destroy the wisdom of the wise;
>>   the intelligence of the intelligent I will frustrate."
>
> Where is the wise man? Where is the scholar? Where is the philosopher of this age? Has not God made foolish the wisdom of the world? For since in the wisdom of God the world through its wisdom did not know him, God was pleased through the foolishness of what was preached to save those who believe (1 Cor. 1:18-21).

In making this indictment, Paul was echoing only what the Greeks themselves had concluded. The philosophers knew that they had been unable to discover God by their philosophy.

The second way Paul explains his decision to know nothing but Christ crucified is the statement that spiritual realities can only be known by God's Spirit. "The man without the Spirit does not accept the things that come from the Spirit of God, for they are foolishness to him, and he cannot understand them, because they are spiritually discerned" (1 Cor. 2:14).

This does not mean that a person cannot have a rational understanding of Christianity or of what the Bible teaches apart from the illumination given by the Spirit. A scholar can understand Christian theology as well as any other branch of knowledge. A philosopher can lecture on the Christian idea of God. A historian can analyze the nature of the Protestant Reformation and describe justification by faith very well. But left to themselves, people like this do not believe what they explain, nor are they saved or changed by it. If they are asked their opinion of what they are explaining, they will say that it is nonsense. It is in this sense that they, not being "spiritual," are unable to understand Christianity.

3. *No one seeks God.* Having spoken of our moral and intellectual failures, Paul moves to man's will and concludes rightly that "no one . . . seeks God."

"But I do seek him," someone might reply. "I have been seeking him all my life. I was born into a Baptist home; but I couldn't find God in my Baptist church. So when I grew old enough I joined a Presbyterian Church. When I couldn't find God there, I became an Episcopalian. Over the years I have attended every kind of church there is. I have been to Lutheran, Pentecostal, Methodist, Bible, and independent churches. But I still haven't found God."

A person like that has not been seeking God. He has been running away from him. The man was probably born into a godly Baptist home. But when God got close to him in his Baptist church, he left it and joined the Presbyterians. When things got hot for him there—God can work even in Presbyterian churches!—he joined the Episcopal church. When God got too close to him in the Episcopal church, he left it for Lutheran, Pentecostal, Methodist, Bible, and independent churches. If he gets to the end of this circle, he will probably look around carefully to see if anyone is looking and then jump in again at the beginning.

This is what sinful human beings are like. So it is no wonder that those who have no righteousness cannot understand spiritual things, and that those who do not seek God fail to appreciate God's grace. They not only fail to appreciate God's grace, they even hate God for it. They resent the suggestion that God needs to be gracious to them. What is incomprehensible is that so many true Christians, who should understand the nature, depth, extent, and horror of their sin, fail to be shocked by it and therefore find grace boring.

MAN'S SPIRITUAL INABILITY

Our culture has taught us that for mankind "all things are possible." So the thought that we need the grace of God in order to get right with God seems wrong to us. We assume that it will always be possible for us to mend our relationships with the Almighty. If it is necessary, we will take care of it ourselves in due time.

Those who think like this fail to appreciate another biblical doctrine: man's spiritual inability or, as it is also sometimes stated, the bondage of man's will. This is the truth behind Paul's statement that there is "no one who seeks God" (Rom. 3:11). The reason no one seeks God is that, apart from the prior work of God in an individual's heart, no one *can* seek God—because no one *wants* to. This matter has been discussed at great length in church history. It was the chief issue in the clash between the great Saint Augustine and the British monk Pelagius; between Martin Luther and the Dutch humanist Erasmus of Rotterdam; and between Jacob Arminius and the followers of John Calvin. However, the deepest and most significant thinking ever done on the subject of the will and its impotence was by Jonathan Edwards in a treatise called "A Careful and Strict Inquiry into the Prevailing Notions of the Freedom of the Will."[5]

The first thing Edwards did was to define the will. We think of the will as that thing in us that makes choices. Edwards saw that this was not accurate and instead defined the will as "that by which *the mind* chooses anything." That may not seem to be much of a difference, but it is a major one. For it means that what we choose is not determined by the will itself (as if it were an entity to itself) but by the mind, which means that our choices are determined by what we think to be the most desirable course of action.

Edwards's second major contribution was his discussion of what he called "motives." He pointed out that the mind is not neutral. It thinks some things are better than other things, and because it thinks some things are better than other things it always chooses the better things. If a person thought one course of action was better than another and yet chose the less desirable alternative, the person would be irrational. This means, to speak properly, that the will is always free. It is free to choose (and always will choose) what the mind thinks best.

But what does the mind think best? Here we get to the heart of the matter. When confronted with God, the mind of a sinner never thinks that following or obeying God is a good choice. His will is free to choose God. Nothing is stopping him. But his mind does not regard submission to God as desirable. Therefore, he turns from God, even when the gospel is most winsomely presented. People do not want God to be sovereign over them. They do not want their sinful natures to be exposed. Their minds are wrong in these judgments, of course. The way they choose is actually the way of alienation and misery, the end of which is death. But human beings think sin is best, which is why they choose it. Therefore, unless God changes the way we think—which he does in some by the miracle of the new birth—our minds always tells us to turn from God—which is precisely what we do.

People who reject this might argue, "But surely the Bible says that anyone who will come to Christ may come to him. Didn't Jesus invite us to come? Didn't Jesus say, 'Whoever comes to me I will never drive away'" (John 6:37)? Yes, that is what Jesus said, but it is beside the point. Certainly, anyone who wants to come to Christ may come to him. That is why Edwards insisted that the will is not bound. But who is it who wills to come? The answer is: No one, except those in whom the Holy Spirit has already performed the entirely irresistible work of the new birth so that, as a result of this miracle, the spiritually blind eyes of the natural man are opened to see God's truth, and the totally depraved mind of the sinner, which in itself has no spiritual understanding, is renewed to embrace the Lord Jesus Christ as Savior. This is teaching that very few professing Christians in our day, including the vast majority of evangelicals, believe or understand, which is another reason, perhaps the major reason, why they find grace boring.

God's Judgment

Most of our contemporaries, even Christians, have lost appreciation for all cause-and-effect links, especially in moral areas. So a judgment of God at the end of human history, when sin will be punished, seems like fantasy to them. Is it fantasy? Or is it actually the most reasonable thing in the universe? We can approach these questions by thinking of Jesus' three great parables of judgment, found in Matthew 25: the parable of the five wise and five foolish virgins; the parable of the talents; and the parable of the sheep and goats. Each makes similar points, so the cumulative effect of these three stories is quite strong.

1. *There will be a future day of reckoning for all people.* This first point is so obvious both from the teaching of the Bible and from our experience of life that it seems almost juvenile to stress it. Yet it must be stressed, if only because most people think in precisely opposite categories. Jesus spoke of judgment being obvious, but most people think of judgment as being the most irrational and least-to-be-anticipated thing in the world.

What do most people think of when one speaks of dying? Most probably do not want to think of it at all; they are afraid of dying, and they are not certain of what, if anything, lies beyond death's door. If they do speak about it, assuming that something does lie beyond this life, most people think of the afterlife in good terms. At the very least they think of something like a continuation of life as we know it. Or, if it will not be that, it must be something better. Very few consider that it may be something worse. They cannot imagine God to be a God of judgment.

Our contemporaries are irrational in this, as they are in other spiritual matters. Ours is an evil world. All sins are not judged in this world, nor are all good deeds rewarded. The righteous do suffer. The guilty do go free. If this is a moral universe, that is, if it is created and ruled by a moral God, then there must be a reckoning hereafter in which the tables are balanced out. The good must prosper and the evil must be punished.

In most theological volumes on eschatology (the last things), there are three great points of emphasis: the return of Christ, the resurrection of the body, and the final judgment. But of the three, the only one that is truly reasonable is the last. There is no reason why Jesus should return again. He came once and was rejected. If he were to write us off and never again give so much as a thought to this planet, it would be completely understandable. It is the same with the resurrection: "Dust you are and to dust you will return"

(Gen. 3:19). If that is all there is, who can complain? We have had our lives. Why should we expect anything more? There is nothing of logical necessity in either of those two matters in and of themselves. But judgment? That is the most logical thing in the universe, and these three stories say quite clearly that there will be a final day of reckoning.

In the first story the bridegroom returns suddenly, and the women who are not ready for his coming are excluded from the marriage feast (Matt. 25:10).

In the story of the servants, the master returns to settle his accounts, and the evil, lazy servant is condemned: "Throw that worthless servant outside, into the darkness, where there will be weeping and gnashing of teeth" (v. 30).

In the final story the king separates the sheep from the goats, sending the wicked "to eternal punishment" and the righteous "to eternal life" (v. 46).

2. *The judgment will be based on our good works or the lack of them.* This is a surprising point for Protestants especially. We have been taught that salvation is by grace through faith apart from works, and here the judgment is on the basis of what people have done or have not done. In the first case it is the failure of the foolish virgins to prepare for the Lord's coming. In the second case it is the disuse of the talents given to the servants by their master. In the third case it is the care or neglect of those who were hungry, thirsty, strangers, naked, sick, or imprisoned. This seems wrong to Protestants because we have been taught that the judgment will be on the basis of whether or not we have believed on Jesus as our Savior.

Salvation is by faith, of course. These stories do not deny that. But they are pointing to something else that is also important, namely, that the faith through which we are saved is not a dead faith. Saving faith must be active. In teaching this, Jesus was one with the apostle James, who said, "What good is it, my brothers, if a man claims to have faith but has no deeds? Can such faith save him? Suppose a brother or sister is without clothes and daily food. If one of you says to him, 'Go, I wish you well; keep warm and well fed,' but does nothing about his physical needs, what good is it? In the same way, faith by itself, if it is not accompanied by action, is dead" (James 2:14-17).

Does that mean we are saved by works after all? Were the Reformers wrong? No, but it is a statement of the necessity of works following faith—if we are truly regenerate. It means that there is an unbreakable link between what we think and what we do. Those who are born again think differently from those who are not, precisely because they have been regenerated; regenerated people will begin to live out the superior moral life of Christ. No one believes on Christ who has not been given a new nature, and although that new nature does not show itself completely all at once, if we are justified, we have it and it will increasingly and inevitably express itself in forgiveness of and service to others, just as God has forgiven and done good to us. We are not justified by works. But if we do not do good works, we are not justified. We are not Christians.

3. *None of our excuses will have any weight before God.* As we read these stories we find that the people who were confronted by the Lord's return made manifold excuses for themselves, just as people make excuses for their wickedness today. The man who had been given one talent and had hidden it in the ground explained that he had not done more because he knew the nature of his master too well: "Master, . . . I knew that you are a hard man, harvesting where you have not sown and gathering where you have not scattered seed. So I was afraid and went out and hid your talent in the ground. See, here is what belongs to you" (Matt. 25:24-25). The man claimed knowledge of his master's character as an excuse for failing to do what his master desired. It was a foolish excuse, but many people today do the same. They use justification theology to excuse their failure to care for others practically. They use knowledge of predestination to excuse their failure to evangelize. They use perseverance as an excuse for being lazy.

The master told the servant that if he were right about his master's character, he should have worked all the harder. He also called him wicked and lazy—wicked because of his unjustified slander, and lazy because that was the actual cause of his zero-growth performance! By those standards, what wicked people must there be in our churches! How lazy some of us must be!

The third story shows another excuse. In that parable the wicked are judged because they have not cared for Christ's brothers. But they reply, "Lord, when did we see you hungry or thirsty or a stranger or needing clothes or sick or in prison, and did not help you?" (v. 44). They complain that they did not see Jesus in those who were needy. To Jesus that is no excuse at all. He says, "Whatever you did not do for one of the least of these, you did not do for me" (v. 45).

You can get away with giving excuses to other people—your boss, your parents, your pastor. But you cannot excuse yourself before God. The apostle Paul wrote that in the day of judgment, "every mouth [will] be silenced and the whole world held accountable to God" (Rom. 3:19). When the Judge takes the bench, there will not be a single protest.

4. *Many who are condemned will be utterly surprised at this outcome.* I have been to a few surprise parties where the person for whom the party was being given was really surprised. Usually they have not been, because they have noticed the clandestine preparations or someone has unwittingly "let the cat out of the bag." But sometimes the surprise has really come off. When I read these parables I realize that there will be a terrible surprise for many on the day of judgment, and it will not be a pretend surprise either. Many will be astounded and utterly dismayed at Christ's judgment.

This is seen in each of these stories. The five women who are left outside knock on the door and call out, "Sir! Sir! Open the door for us!" They are amazed when the door is not opened. The man who had buried the talent is equally surprised. So also with the "goats," who have failed to serve others as they think they would have served Christ. They say, "When did we see you hungry or thirsty or a stranger or needing clothes or sick or in prison, and did not help you?" (v. 44). They mean that they would have done everything necessary if they had only seen Christ, but since they did not see him they cannot imagine why they are being judged. Instead of judgment, each of these persons expected to be rewarded.

Here, I suppose, is the perfect portrait of the visible but unbelieving church, a picture of many who in their lifetime called out, "Lord, Lord," but did not do the things Jesus said and ultimately perished. We would not dare say this if the Lord had not said it first, but on his authority we must say that many who worship in apparently Christian congregations, who consider themselves good Christians, supposing that all is well with their souls, will be utterly surprised by God's judgment. If people like this will be shut out from God's presence, ought we not to do as Peter says and "make [our] calling and election sure" (2 Pet. 1:10)? Peter tells how it must be done. He says to add goodness to faith, knowledge to goodness, self-control to knowledge, perseverance to self-control, godliness to perseverance, brotherly kindness to godliness, and love to brotherly kindness (vv. 5-7), concluding, "If you *do* these things, you will never fall, and you will receive a rich welcome into the eternal kingdom of our Lord and Savior Jesus Christ" (vv. 10-11). The emphasis is on "do"!

GOD'S SOVEREIGN FREEDOM

In this day of multiple human "rights," most people wrongly assume that God owes us something—salvation or at least a chance at salvation. But in Packer's discussion of grace, which we referenced at the beginning of this chapter, the author notes rightly that God does not owe us anything. He shows astonishing favor to many—that is what grace means—but he does not have to. If he were obliged to be gracious, grace would no longer be grace and salvation would be based on human merit rather than being *sola gratia*.[6]

When we say that God is not obligated to be gracious we are talking about sovereign grace, and when we are speaking about sovereign grace there is no better Bible passage to study than Ephesians 1. Most Christians are aware of Paul's teaching about grace in Ephesians 2. In fact, many have memorized Ephesians 2:8-9, which describes grace. What most do not realize is that the meaning of grace in those verses has already been defined by what has been said about grace in chapter 1. Chapter 1 is about God's sovereign grace from the beginning to the end.

What is the difference between Ephesians 1 and 2? Both chapters use the word *grace* three times. But chapter 1 looks at the subject from God's point of view, showing that we are saved because of what God has willed, while chapter 2 looks at the subject from our perspective, showing how these prior decrees of God impact the individual believer. The important thing is that Paul begins with God. What is more, in beginning with God he highlights the role of each person of the Trinity in this work.

1. *The role of God the Father: election.* "He chose us in him before the creation of the world to be holy and blameless in his sight. In love he predestined us to be adopted as his sons through Jesus Christ, in accordance with his pleasure and will—to the praise of his glorious grace, which he has freely given us in the One he loves" (Eph. 1:4-6). These verses are one of the strongest expressions of sovereign grace in Scripture, for they teach that the blessings of salvation come to some people because God has determined from before the creation of the world to give these blessings to these people—and for that reason only.

Many people today do not like this doctrine because they think it is not just. Some deny it outright. Some admit it but deny its effect by saying that the choice is based on God's foreknowledge—as if there were anything good in us for God to foresee, apart from his having previously determined to put it there. Some ignore the doctrine. But it is hard to ignore election, since it is found throughout the Bible and in so many critical passages. Without God's prior election of sinners to salvation, grace is emptied of its meaning.

2. *The role of God the Son: redemption.* Election is not the only thing God has done as an expression of his grace in salvation. Following the Trinitarian pattern of this chapter, we come next to the doctrine of redemption. What God has done through Jesus Christ is to redeem his elect or chosen people, which also flows from unmerited or utterly sovereign grace. "In him we have redemption through his blood, the forgiveness of sins, in accor-

dance with the riches of God's grace that he lavished on us with all wisdom and understanding" (Eph. 1:7-8).

The reason redemption is particularly associated with Jesus Christ is that redemption is a commercial term meaning "to buy in the marketplace so that the object or person purchased might be freed from it," and Jesus did this buying and liberating work for us by dying in our place. To carry the illustration through, we are pictured as slaves to sin, unable to free ourselves from sin's bondage and the world's grasp. Indeed, instead of freeing us, the world joyfully gambles for our bodies and souls. It offers its alluring currency—fame, sex, pleasure, power, wealth. For these things millions sell their eternal souls and perish. But Jesus enters the marketplace as our Redeemer. Jesus bids the price of his blood. God says, "Sold to Jesus, for the price of his blood!" There is no higher bid than that. So we become his possession forever.

The apostle Peter wrote, "It was not with perishable things such as silver or gold that you were redeemed from the empty way of life handed down to you from your forefathers, but with the precious blood of Christ, a lamb without blemish or defect" (1 Pet. 1:18-19). Charles Wesley expressed it poetically:

> Long my imprisoned spirit lay
> Fast bound in sin and nature's night;
> Thine eye diffused a quick'ning ray;
> I woke, the dungeon flamed with light;
> My chains fell off, my heart was free;
> I rose, went forth, and followed thee.[7]

3. *The role of God the Holy Spirit: effectual calling.* The third expression of God's sovereign grace in our salvation emphasized in Ephesians 1 is the work of the Holy Spirit, who applies to the individual the salvation planned by God the Father and achieved by God the Son. "In him we were also chosen, having been predestined according to the plan of him who works out everything in conformity with the purpose of his will, in order that we, who

were the first to hope in Christ, might be for the praise of his glory. And you also were included in Christ when you heard the word of truth, the gospel of your salvation. Having believed, you were marked in him with a seal, the promised Holy Spirit, who is a deposit guaranteeing our inheritance until the redemption of those who are God's possession—to the praise of his glory" (Eph. 1:11-14).

At first glance the word "chosen" in verse 11 seems to be describing the same thing as Paul's words about the Father's choice in verse 4, that is, election. But the idea is actually different. In verse 4 the predestining choice of the Father stands before everything. In verse 11, "chosen" refers to what theologians term the Holy Spirit's effective call, which follows from and is determined by the exercise of God's sovereign will in election.

The greatest biblical picture of the grace of God calling a dead sinner to life is probably Jesus' raising of Lazarus, recorded in John 11. When Jesus returned to Bethany at the request of the dead man's sisters, he was told that Lazarus had been dead for four days and that he was already putrefying: "'But Lord,' said Martha, . . . 'by this time there is a bad odor, for he has been there four days'" (v. 39). What a graphic description of the state of our moral and spiritual decay because of sin! Dead, decaying, stinking, hopeless. There was nothing anyone could do for Lazarus in this dead condition. His situation was not merely serious or grim; it was hopeless.

But not to God! "With God all things are possible" (Matt. 19:26). Therefore, having prayed, Jesus called, "Lazarus, come out!" (John 11:43), and the call of Jesus brought life to the dead man, just as the voice of God brought the entire universe into being from nothing.

That is what the Holy Spirit does to moribund sinners today. God's Spirit works through the preaching of the Bible to call to faith those he has previously chosen for salvation and for whom Jesus specifically died. Apart from those three gracious actions—the act of God in electing, the work of Christ in dying, and the operation of the Holy Spirit in calling—there would be no salvation for anyone. But because of those actions—because of God's sovereign grace—even the worst of blaspheming rebels may be turned from his or her folly and may find Christ.

AMAZING GRACE

Whenever I come to a tremendous word like *grace,* one of the things I do is look in hymn books to see what has been written about it by Christians who have gone before me. When I did that for grace, consulting the *Trinity Hymnal,* the book we use in our church, I was surprised by the many words for grace and the many varieties of grace that were listed. The *Trinity Hymnal* lists hymns about grace under the following headings: converting grace, the covenant of grace, efficacious grace, the fullness of grace, magnified grace, refreshing grace, regenerating grace, sanctifying grace, saving grace, and sovereign grace. It also has combined listings, such as: the love and grace of God, the love and grace of Christ, the love and grace of the Holy Spirit, and salvation by grace.

In addition, there are the phrases used in the hymns themselves, such as: abounding grace, abundant grace, amazing grace, boundless grace, fountain of grace, God of grace, indelible grace, marvelous grace, matchless grace, overflowing grace, pardoning grace, plenteous grace, unfailing grace, immeasurable grace, wonderful grace, the word of grace, grace all sufficient, and grace alone.

Did you know that Francis Scott Key, the author of the national anthem of the United States, also wrote an important hymn about grace?

> Praise the grace whose threats alarmed thee,
> Roused thee from thy fatal ease,
> Praise the grace whose promise warmed thee,
> Praise the grace that whispered peace.[8]

My favorite hymn, as least as far as the words go, was written by Samuel Davies, a Presbyterian minister and former president of Princeton University:

Great God of wonders! All thy ways
Are worthy of thyself—divine:
And the bright glories of thy grace
Among thine other wonders shine;
Who is a pardoning God like thee?
Or who has grace so rich and free?[9]

Theologians speak of common grace, electing grace, irresistible grace, persevering grace, prevenient grace, pursuing grace, and saving grace. Yet even these terms do not exhaust the Christian terminology.

At the beginning of this chapter we took note of John Newton (1725–1807). Newton was raised in a Christian home in which he was taught verses of the Bible, but his mother died when he was only six years old and he was sent to live with a relative who hated the Bible and mocked Christianity. Newton ran away to sea. He was wild in those years and was known for being able to swear for two hours without repeating himself. He was forced to enlist in the British navy, but he deserted, was captured, and was beaten publicly as a punishment. Eventually Newton got into the merchant marine and went to Africa. In his memoirs he wrote that he went to Africa for one reason only, "that I might sin my fill."

Newton fell in with a Portuguese slave trader, in whose home he was cruelly treated. This man often went away on slaving expeditions, and when he was gone his power passed to his African wife, the chief woman of his harem. She hated all white men and vented her hatred on Newton. He says that for months he was forced to grovel in the dirt, eating his food from the ground like a dog. He was beaten mercilessly if he touched it. In time, thin and emaciated, Newton made his way to the sea, where he was picked up by a British ship making its way up the coast to England.

When the captain of the ship learned that the young man knew something about navigation as a result of being in the British Navy, he made him a ship's mate. But even then Newton fell into trouble. One day, when the captain was ashore, Newton broke out the ship's supply of rum and got the crew drunk. He was so drunk himself that when the captain returned and struck him on the head, Newton fell overboard and would have drowned if one of the sailors had not quickly hauled him back on board.

Near the end of one voyage, as they were approaching Scotland, the ship ran into bad weather and was blown off course. Water poured in, and the ship began to sink. The young profligate was sent down into the hold to pump water. The storm lasted for days. Newton was terrified. He was sure the ship would sink and he would drown. But in the hold of the ship, as he desperately pumped water, the God of all grace, whom he had tried to forget but who had never forgotten him, brought to his mind Bible verses he had learned in his home as a child. The way of salvation opened up to him. He was born again and deeply transformed. Much later, when he was again in England, Newton began to study theology and eventually became a preacher, first in a little town called Olney and later in London.

Of this storm William Cowper, the British poet who became a fast personal friend of Newton and lived with him for several years, wrote:

> God moves in a mysterious way,
>   His wonders to perform;
> He plants his footsteps in the sea
>   And rides upon the storm.[10]

And so he does! Newton was a great preacher of grace, for he had learned that where sin increased, grace abounded all the more (Rom. 5:20). He is proof that the grace of God is sufficient to save anybody, and that he saves them by grace alone.

SIX

❖

Faith Alone

Since grace is the source of the life that is mine—
And faith is a gift from on high—
I'll boast in my Savior, all merit decline,
And glorify God 'til I die.

The Alliance of Confessing Evangelicals has called evangelicals to repent of their worldliness and to recover the great doctrines of the Bible, as the Reformers did in the sixteenth century. In the preceding three chapters we have been exploring what that might mean. In those chapters we looked at three of the most central doctrines: "Scripture alone," "Christ alone," and "grace alone." We will be looking at "glory to God alone" in the chapter that follows this.

But I must say here that there is no place at which our recovery needs to begin more rigorously than with the doctrine of justification by faith, since this is what the Reformers called the "material principle" of all theology. They called the doctrine of Scripture alone the "formal principle" because it is from the Bible that we derive our theology. We believe what we believe because we find it in the Bible. But then, having established the sole source from which our doctrine comes, the Reformers turned to justification and called it the "material principle," because it involves the very matter, substance, or heart of what any man or woman must understand and believe to be saved.

Statements about the importance and centrality of justification by faith are found throughout the Reformers' writings. John Calvin, the spiritual father of the Presbyterian and Reformed churches and the most systematic of the Reformation theologians, spoke of justification as "the main hinge on which salvation turns."[1]

Thomas Cranmer was the chief architect of the Church of England, the major figure behind the *Book of Common Prayer.* He believed that justification is "the strong rock and foundation of Christian religion," declaring that "whosoever denieth [this doctrine] is not to be counted for a true Christian man . . . but for an adversary of Christ."[2]

Thomas Watson was one of the finest of the English Puritans and one of their most readable writers. He said that "justification is the very hinge and pillar of Christianity. An error about justification is dangerous, like a defect in a foundation. Justification by Christ is a spring of the water of life. To have the poison of corrupt doctrine cast into this spring is damnable."[3]

Martin Luther was the first of all the Reformers, the founder of the Lutheran churches, and one of the most outspoken of any in this volatile but determinative period. Luther said, "When the article of justification has fallen, everything has fallen. . . . This is the chief article from which all other doctrines have flowed. . . . It alone begets, nourishes, builds, preserves, and defends the church of God; and without it the church of God cannot exist for one hour." He maintained that justification is "the master and prince, the lord, the ruler, and the judge over all kinds of doctrines."[4]

These statements are not exaggerations. They are simple truth, because justification is God's answer to the most important of all human questions: How can a man or a woman become right with God? We are not right with God in ourselves. On the contrary, we are in dreadful trouble with God. We are under his wrath for our sins. So either we must become right with God or we must perish eternally. If the evangelical church loses this doctrine, as it is in the process of doing, it will fall, as Luther said. Evangelical churches are falling. And this means that they are not only losing their soul, they are ceasing to be true churches. They are becoming something that is actually non-Christian.

AN IMAGE FROM THE LAW COURTS

We need, then, to look carefully at what justification by faith means, and to do that we can turn to a great passage of Scripture in which the apostle Paul unfolds in powerful and definitive language what God the Father has done in Jesus Christ for our salvation. It is from Romans 3, after Paul has analyzed the rebellion of the race against the Creator and has shown how all alike are without hope apart from God's grace. This, says Paul, is because "there is no one righteous, . . . no one who understands, no one who seeks God" (vv. 10-11). He writes:

> But now a righteousness from God, apart from law, has been made known, to which the Law and the Prophets testify. This righteousness from God comes through faith in Jesus Christ to all who believe. There is no difference, for all have sinned and fall short of the glory of God, and are justified freely by his grace through the redemption that came by Christ Jesus. God presented him as a sacrifice of atonement, through faith in his blood (Rom. 3:21-25).

This passage introduces several key terms. *Redemption* is one. It was discussed in the last chapter. It concerns buying and selling and emphasizes the price Jesus paid for our deliverance. Because the word was often used for the buying of slaves, it has overtones of delivering believers in Christ from sin's slavery. *Propitiation* ("a sacrifice of atonement," NIV) is another key term. We looked at it in chapter 4. It is borrowed from the world of ancient religion, where it describes the sacrifice by which the wrath of God toward sinners is turned aside. In ancient times people thought they could turn God's wrath away by themselves, presenting sacrifices commensurate with their transgressions. But although the idea is the same, in Christianity it is understood that no mere human being can placate or turn aside God's wrath. Only God can do that, and that is precisely what he has done through the only sufficient sacrifice of Christ.

What about *justification?* This word comes from the world of the law courts and describes the act of a judge in acquitting an accused person. Leon Morris says rightly that "justification . . . is a legal term indicating the process of declaring righteous."[5]

It is important to note the words "acquit" and "declare." This is because the single most serious error in trying to understand justification is to suppose that it means "to make righteous" in the sense of actually producing righteousness in the one justified. It is true that an actual righteousness does follow from justification— so closely that we are right to say that if it does not follow, the person is not justified. But justification in itself does not refer to this change. The English word might lead us to think so. It is composed of the two Latin words *justus,* meaning "just" or "righteous," and *facio,* meaning "to make." So at first glance justification seems to mean "to make righteous." But that is not the right idea. The word only indicates that the person involved has a right standing before the bar of God's justice. It does not indicate how he or she got that way, which is why the other terms which refer to the work of Jesus Christ on our behalf are also necessary.

This is where Martin Luther struggled. According to an understanding of justification based on the meaning of the Latin word, which is what he found in his Latin Vulgate Bible, justification is a process through which the individual becomes intrinsically holy. This seemed to make sense, because God cannot declare a person to be just if the person is not just. God does not play word games. Therefore, the person must become just, and it is only after that happens that God can declare the person to be justified. But how does a person become just? The medieval church replied that it is by the sacraments. And if that is not sufficient, there is always purgatory, where the punishment for sins that have not been adequately confessed and forgiven may be worked off and a true intrinsic righteousness may be attained.

Luther tried to do it. He had entered the monastery of the Augustinian order at Erfurt on August 17, 1505, as he said, "in order to save my soul," and he became a model monk in his duties. He labored long in prayer. He fasted and even beat his body to subdue the flesh. Above all, he was rigorous in doing penance, entering the confessional for hours at a time and so wearying his confessors that they would eventually tell him to return to his cell and not come back until he had committed a sin worth confessing.

Luther later said of himself in a letter to the Duke of Saxony, "I was indeed a pious monk and followed the rules of my order more strictly than I can express. If ever a monk could obtain heaven by his monkish works, I should certainly have been entitled to it. Of this all the friars who have known me can testify. If it had continued much longer, I should have carried my mortification even to death, by means of my watchings, prayers, reading and other labors."[6] But Luther found no peace through these exercises. The wisdom of his order instructed him to satisfy God's demand for righteousness by doing good works. "But what works can come from a heart like mine?" thought Luther. "How can I stand before the holiness of my Judge with works polluted in their very source?"[7]

Fortunately, Luther had a wise father superior named John Staupitz, who set him to studying the Bible. And as he studied the Bible, particularly the book of Romans, Luther discovered that the accepted understanding of justification was mistaken. The Greek term, which is quite different from the Latin translation, does not refer to an intrinsic change in the individual at all, but rather to a declaration made by God. It is what a judge does in court when he declares a person to be in a right standing before the law.

Justification is the opposite of condemnation. When a plaintiff stands in a wrong relationship to the law, he or she is condemned by the judge. Condemnation does not make the person guilty. He or she is only declared to be so. In the same way, in justification the person is declared to be just or in a right relationship to the law, but not made righteous. A person *could* be declared righteous on the basis of his or her own righteousness; such a one would actually be innocent. But in salvation, since we have no righteousness of our own and are not innocent, we are declared righteous solely on the ground of Christ's atonement for our sin and Christ's righteousness imputed to us. Luther later said that when he discovered that and had trusted in the Christ who had paid the full price of his salvation, it was as if he passed through the gates of heaven to paradise.

A WELL-DEVELOPED DOCTRINE

Most Christians know the words "justification by faith," and most understand that "by faith" means "by faith alone" (*sola fide*). Yet we have also heard the doctrine described as "justification by grace alone" (*sola gratia*). Which leads us to ask: Which is it? Is it justification by faith alone, or is it justification by grace alone? The answer, of course, is that it is both, since both are parts of the same reality. In fact, to be complete we need to add the other Reformation *sola,* "Christ alone" (*solus Christus*), since it is only because of Christ and his work that God can justify the ungodly. A full definition is this:

> Justification is an act of God by which he declares sinners to be righteous by grace alone through faith alone because of Christ alone.

That is exactly what Paul is teaching in Romans 3:21-26, of course, because the verses include each of those elements. They refer to a righteousness that is not our own but is instead a righteousness from God revealed from heaven (v. 21). They speak of God's grace ("justified freely by his grace," v. 24). They talk about faith; the word appears eight times in verses 21-31. And all this is said to be possible because of Christ. "This righteousness from God comes through faith in Jesus Christ" (v. 22), and we are "justified freely by his grace through the redemption that came by Christ Jesus" (v. 24).

Let's take that definition one step at a time, as John R. W. Stott does in his treatment of it in *The Cross of Christ.*[8]

1. *The source of our justification is the grace of God (v. 24).* Since "there is no one righteous, not even one" (Rom. 3:10), it is clear

that no one can make or "declare" himself or herself "righteous" (v. 20). How, then, is salvation possible? It is possible only if God does the work for us—which is what "grace" means, since we do not deserve God's working. In fact, we do not even seek it. Not only is there "no one righteous" and "no one who understands" (Rom. 3:10, 11). It is also the case that there "is no one who seeks God" (v. 11). If it were not for the inexplicable grace of God, utterly unsought and utterly unmerited, no one would be justified.

2. *The ground of our justification is the work of Christ (v. 25).* This is why Paul includes "propitiation" and "redemption" in this powerful paragraph summary of the gospel—"redemption" in verse 24, and "propitiation" ("sacrifice of atonement") in verse 25. This pivotal doctrine is being lost in our day, but it was not always held in such low esteem. It was precious to Charles Haddon Spurgeon, to name just one past warrior. In fact, it was the means of his conversion. Here is how he tells it:

> When I was under the hand of the Holy Spirit, under conviction of sin, I had a clear and sharp sense of the justice of God. Sin, whatever it might be to other people, became to me an intolerable burden. . . . I knew myself to be so horribly guilty that I remember feeling that if God did not punish me for sin he ought to do so. I felt that the Judge of all the earth ought to condemn such sin as mine. . . . I had upon my mind a deep concern for the honor of God's name, and the integrity of his moral government. I felt that it would not satisfy my conscience if I could be forgiven unjustly. The sin I had committed must be punished. But then there was the question how God could be just, and yet justify me who had been so guilty. . . . I was worried and wearied with this question; neither could I see any answer to it. Certainly, I could never have invented an answer which would have satisfied my conscience.

But then, as the great Baptist preacher recounted, light dawned on his soul. He saw that

Jesus has borne the death penalty on our behalf. . . . Why did
he suffer, if not to turn aside the penalty from us? If, then, he
turned it aside by his death, it is turned aside, and those who
believe in him need not fear it. It must be so, that since expiation is made, God is able to forgive without shaking the basis
of his throne.[9]

That is a genuine conversion, and it is one reason at least why
Spurgeon became such a powerful Bible teacher and evangelist. He
knew the power of the gospel of justification by the grace of God,
received by faith alone, and he was eager to proclaim this Good
News to people who were perishing.

When Paul wrote about God leaving "the sins committed
beforehand unpunished" and about demonstrating "his justice at
the present time" (Rom. 3:25, 26), he was dealing with a temporal
problem, acknowledging that before the Incarnation and death of
Christ there had been something like a stain on God's name. God
had been refusing to condemn and instead had actually been justi-
fying sinful men and women—men like Abraham, who was willing to compromise his wife's honor to save his own life; Moses, who
killed an Egyptian; David, who committed adultery with Bathsheba
and then murdered her husband Uriah to cover up the adultery;
and women like Rahab, the prostitute of Jericho. God had been saving these people. When they died he did not send them to hell. It
would seem to anyone looking on that God had been passing over
their sins—forgiving them, yes, but unjustly.

We can understand how God might want to overlook the sins
of these people. We would do the same. Who would want to send
anyone to hell? We can understand how God might be compas-
sionate. But how could God do that and be just? It would seem that
God must either be forgiving and unjust, or just and unforgiving.
All things are possible for God, however. In these words Paul is
explaining that, in the death of Christ, God's name has been vindi-
cated, since it is now understood that it was on the ground of
Christ's future death that God had been just when he justified (and
continues to justify) the ungodly.

3. *The means of our justification is faith* (vv. 25-26). Finally, faith is the channel by which justification comes to us or actually becomes ours. Faith is not a good work. It is necessary and essential. But it is not a good work. In fact, it is not a work at all. It is God's gift, as Paul makes clear in Ephesians 2:8-9: "It is by grace you have been saved, through faith—and this not from yourselves, it is the gift of God—not by works, so that no one can boast." But although it is only the channel by which we are justified, it is also the *only* channel. This is what is meant by *sola fide* ("faith alone"). If faith is merely receiving what God has done for us, then it is by faith alone that we are justified—all other acts or works being excluded by definition.

LEST WE FORGET *SOLA FIDE*

In the previous chapters we saw how many of today's evangelicals are forgetting *solus Christus* by marginalizing Christ and his Cross. They retain Jesus as an example and helper, but they have forgotten him as an atoning sacrifice for sin. They have destroyed *sola gratia* by clinging to their own human merit ("God helps those who help themselves") and by insisting that God owes everyone at least a chance to be saved ("If God does not give everybody a chance to be saved, he is not fair"). What about *sola fide?* How are we forgetting faith alone? We are doing so by subtracting from it, by making faith less than what the Bible says it is and must be.

Clearly, we must have faith. We can hardly miss that in Romans 3:21-31. In those verses Paul says: "This righteousness of God comes through *faith* in Jesus Christ to all who believe" (v. 22). He argues that "God presented him as a sacrifice of atonement, through *faith* in his blood" (v. 25). He teaches that God "justifies those who have *faith* in Jesus" (v. 26). He maintains that "a man is justified by *faith* apart from observing the law" (v. 28). He concludes that "there is only one God, who will justify the circumcised by *faith* and the uncircumcised through that same *faith*" (v. 30). Clearly, faith is essential.

But what is faith? For many evangelicals faith is only a mental assent to certain doctrines. It is something we exercise once at the start of our Christian lives, after which we can live more or less in any way we please. It does not matter in terms of our salvation whether or not this "faith" makes a difference. Some evangelicals even teach that a person could be saved and secure if he or she possessed a dead or dying faith or, incredible as this seems, if he or she apostatizes, denying Jesus.

In contrast to such an eviscerated faith, throughout church history most Bible teachers have insisted that saving, biblical faith has three elements: "knowledge, belief, and trust," as Spurgeon put it; "awareness, assent, and commitment," as D. Martyn Lloyd-Jones said; or *notitia, assensus,* and *fiducia,* to use the Latin terminology.

1. *The first element is* notitia, *or knowledge.* We begin with "knowledge of the truth (or "content")," because faith starts here. Faith without content is no true faith at all. R. C. Sproul says rightly, "I cannot have God in my heart if he is not in my head. Before I can believe *in,* I must believe *that.*"[10] Or as John Gerstner, one of Sproul's teachers, often said, "Nothing can enter the sanctuary of the heart unless it first passes through the vestibule of the mind."

Of the writers on faith, Calvin is perhaps strongest on this point, because he found it necessary to oppose a serious error about faith that had developed in the teaching of the medieval church. In the years before the Reformation, the church had neglected to teach the Scriptures to the people. So most people, even the clergy, were ignorant of the gospel. How were such ignorant persons to be saved? The church answered that it was by an "implicit" faith. That is, it was not necessary for the communicant actually to know anything. All he or she had to do was trust the church implicitly. The church and its teachings were right, even if people did not know what those right teachings were; those people would be all right too, if they just believed or trusted the church.

The situation reminds me of a contemporary story in which a man was being interviewed by a group of church officers before being taken into membership. They asked him what he believed about salvation, and he replied that he believed what the church believed.

"What does the church believe?" they probed.

"The church believes what I believe," he answered.

The committee was a bit exasperated by this time. But they tried again: "Just what do you and the church believe?"

The man thought this over for a moment and then replied, "We believe the same thing."

Calvin argued that "the object of faith is Christ" and that "faith rests upon knowledge, not upon pious ignorance." He wrote:

> We do not obtain salvation either because we are prepared to embrace as true whatever the church has prescribed, or because we turn over to it the task of inquiring and knowing. But we do so when we know that God is our merciful Father, because of reconciliation effected through Christ (2 Cor. 5:18, 19), and that Christ has been given to us as righteousness, sanctification and life. By this knowledge, I say, not by submission of our feeling, do we obtain entry into the Kingdom of Heaven.[11]

2. *The second element is* assensus, *or assent.* It is what Spurgeon called "belief." The idea here is that, important as is the biblical content of faith—the point Calvin stressed so strongly—it is nevertheless possible to know this content well and still be lost—if the teaching has not touched the individual to the point of his or her actually agreeing with it. When I was studying English literature in college I had many professors who understood and were able thoroughly to explain Christian doctrine, since it is so strong in the literature. But they did not believe it. They did not have faith in this second sense.

An illustration of what this second element might mean is the conversion of John Wesley in 1738. The great Methodist evangelist had been an active preacher before his conversion. He knew Christian doctrine, but it had not affected him at a personal level. He had believed, in a sense. But he did not really love Christ or trust him personally. However, one evening he went to a little meeting in Aldersgate Street in London, where someone was reading Luther's "Preface" to the Epistle to the Romans, and Wesley was converted. He wrote, "About a quarter before nine, while he was describing the change which God works in the heart through faith in Christ, I felt my heart strangely warmed. I felt I did trust in Christ, Christ alone for my salvation. And an assurance was given me that he had taken away *my* sins, even *mine,* and saved *me* from the law of sin and death."[12]

Some might argue that Wesley had been saved before this and only came to know it at this point. That may be possible. But Wesley himself testified that this "warming of the heart" was an important part of what is meant by trusting Christ.

Here is how Calvin put it, following a long section dealing with the matter of faith's content: "It now remains to pour into the heart itself what the mind has absorbed. For the Word of God is not received by faith if it flits about in the top of the brain, but when it takes root in the depth of the heart that it may be an invincible defense to withstand and drive off all the stratagems of temptation."[13]

3. *The third element is* fiducia, *or trust and commitment.* The third element of faith, which Spurgeon calls "trust" and Lloyd-Jones calls "commitment," is a real yielding of oneself to Christ which goes beyond knowledge, however full or accurate that knowledge may be, and even beyond agreeing with or being personally moved by the gospel. This must be the case, because even the devils believe in the first two, limited senses. They know what the Bible teaches; they know that it is true. But they are not saved. James was acknowledging this when he described some persons' inadequate faith by writing, "You believe that there is one God. Good! Even the demons believe that—and shudder" (James 2:19). In other words, believing the truths of Christianity itself, if we do not go on to this third necessary element, only qualifies one to be a demon!

Commitment is the point at which we pass over the line from belonging (as we think) to ourselves and become the Lord's true disciples. It is what was seen in Thomas when he fell at Jesus' feet in worship, exclaiming, "My Lord and my God!" (John 20:28).

We can also say this by pointing out that *fiducia,* the third element of faith, involves a radical change of values. Let's take the case of the chief demon, Satan. Satan has the *notitia;* he knows the gospel. He also believes the gospel in the sense that he knows that it is true; in this sense he has the *assensus*. But Satan resists Christ. He is opposed to all he represents. He despises Christ. Therefore, Satan does not have faith in Jesus in a saving sense. For Satan to be saved he would have to have a change in values from passionate hatred to a love of Christ, from passive indifference to a passionate pursuit of salvation. The third element of faith produces such a change, which is why the born-again person now pursues intensely what he or she previously despised. Before, the person saw nothing that was desirable about Jesus. Now, the person cannot imagine life without him.

This is why in Jesus' parables the man who discovered the treasure in the field "went and sold all he had and bought that field" (Matt. 13:44), and why the merchant also "sold everything he had" to purchase the pearl of great price (v. 46). It is why Jesus said, "From the days of John the Baptist until now, the kingdom of heaven has been forcefully advancing, and forceful men lay hold of it" (Matt. 11:12). They lay hold of it because they cannot imagine it to be any other way. Nothing will keep them from what they have found to be the greatest of all treasures.

THE NEW FORM OF AN OLD ERROR

Unfortunately, there is a sizeable segment of the evangelical church that disagrees with the need for these three elements. It restricts the confession "Jesus is Lord" to the belief that Jesus is a divine Savior and explicitly eliminates any idea that Jesus must be Lord of our lives for us to be Christians. It teaches that a person can be a Christian without being a follower of Jesus Christ. It reduces the gospel to the mere fact of Christ's having died for sinners; requires of sinners only that they acknowledge this by the barest kind of intellectual assent, quite apart from any repentance or turning from sin; and then assures them of their eternal security when they may very well not even be born again. This view bends true biblical faith beyond recognition and offers a false assurance to people who may have given verbal assent to this reductionist type of Christianity but who are not in God's family. Those who take this position call the Reformed understanding of the gospel "Lordship salvation" and dismiss it as heresy.

Few theological positions, orthodox or not, are without precedent. In this case, the view I am talking about is that of the eighteenth-century Scottish eccentric Robert Sandeman, who taught that everyone who is persuaded that Jesus actually died for sin as testified by the apostles is justified, regardless of any change in his or her life. The view is known by his name, Sandemanianism. However, this old error has appeared in new form in our day largely through the influence of various professors at Dallas Theological Seminary.

One who has taught it is Charles Caldwell Ryrie, editor of the popular *Ryrie Study Bible*. The most extreme proponent of the view is Zane C. Hodges, who has defended it in three works titled *The Gospel Under Siege; Dead Faith: What Is It?* and *Absolutely Free!*[14] Scores of other people also think this way, even though they may not consciously trace their views to the "Dallas doctrine." This doctrine has been brought to the surface by being challenged by John MacArthur in a book called *The Gospel According to Jesus*.[15]

Charles Ryrie, Zane Hodges, and those who think like them want to preserve the purity of the gospel. That is to their considerable credit. They are children of the Reformation in that they believe in justification by faith apart from works and want to guard the gospel from anything that might contaminate it. The reason they oppose a demand for repentance, discipleship, or a walk that gives evidence of an inward spiritual change is that they regard this as adding works to faith—which, as we all know, is a false gospel.

Again, they want to affirm the doctrine of eternal security, since that too is a Reformation distinctive. They argue that if salvation depends in any way on repenting of sin, commitment, following Jesus Christ as Lord, or behavioral change, then assurance is destroyed, because we all sin. In fact, one of the reasons that this teaching eliminates obedience from the essence of saving faith is to include as Christians professing believers whose lives are filled with sin. "If only committed people are saved people," writes Charles

Ryrie, "then where is there room for carnal Christians?"[16] Where indeed?

Clearly there is an error at this point, and part of it is the doctrine of the "carnal Christian" itself. "Carnal" is not a biblical category for weak Christians. Where the term occurs in Paul's writings, it means an unregenerated person, an unbeliever (see Rom. 8:5-11). Even in 1 Corinthians 3, where Christians are said to be acting in a "worldly" (carnal) way, the point is only that they are acting as if they were not Christians, which must not be. They need to stop that and begin to behave as what they really are.

There are four other areas in which this faulty understanding of the gospel is mistaken:

1. *The meaning of faith.* This is the error I am most concerned about here. Ryrie says, "The message of faith only and the message of faith plus commitment of life cannot both be the gospel; therefore, one of them is a false gospel and comes under the curse of perverting the gospel or preaching another gospel (Gal. 1:6-9)."[17] But this argument fudges on the definition of true faith. If saving faith does not include trust or commitment, then to insist on trust or commitment *is* a false gospel. On the other hand, if faith *includes* trust and commitment, as the greatest theologians of the church have always claimed it does, then to insist on commitment is not to add to faith but only to insist that faith be true faith. That is a critical point, because a false faith, an imitation faith, or a dead faith will save no one.

2. *The need for repentance.* The Dallas school speaks of repentance, but because it does not want to acknowledge a need for behavioral change, it redefines repentance to mean only a "change of mind" concerning who Jesus is, irrespective of any reference to sin. G. Michael Cocoris writes, "The Bible requires repentance for salvation, but repentance does not mean to turn from sin, nor a change in one's conduct. Those are the fruits of repentance. Biblical repentance is a change of mind or attitude concerning either God, Christ, dead works or sin."[18]

But that is not what the Bible means by repentance, and it is certainly not what the Reformers meant. The Bible's use of this important word implies a change of life direction, specifically, a turning from sin. It is the flip side of faith. In conversion we turn *from* sin, which is repentance; and we turn *to* Jesus, which is faith. Conversion itself means "to turn around." That means that we need to turn a full one hundred and eighty degrees. Even more, we need to do it again and again as God brings specific sins to our minds. This is why Martin Luther wrote in the very first of the "Ninety-five Theses," which he posted on the door of the Castle Church at Wittenberg, "When the Lord Jesus Christ told his people to 'repent,' he meant that all of life is to be characterized by repentance."

3. *The demand for discipleship.* The Dallas school divorces salvation from discipleship, thus preserving the school's doctrine of the "carnal Christian." It describes discipleship as something that follows conversion but is separate from it. But Jesus did not make following after him a second step. He defined salvation as discipleship. That is, he did not call people to some bare intellectual assent to who he was, but rather, to become his disciples. He was speaking of salvation when he said, "If anyone would come after me, he must deny himself and take up his cross daily and follow me. For whoever wants to save his life will lose it, but whoever loses his life for me will save it" (Luke 9:23-24).

Several years ago I wrote a book to explore the meaning of Jesus' call to discipleship, in which at one place I examined the matter of its cost. I found that Jesus always stressed the cost of coming to him. He never said anything to suggest even remotely that a person could come to him as Savior and remain unchanged. That insight changed me. I said in the book that if I had been asked earlier what minimum amount of doctrine a person needed to know in order to become a Christian or what minimum price he would have to pay to follow Jesus, I would probably have replied as many still do: Very little. I would not have stressed Christ's demands. But now I say, "The minimum amount a person must believe to be a Christian is *everything,* and the minimum amount a person must give is *all.* You cannot hold back even a fraction of a percentage of yourself. Every sin must be abandoned. Every false thought must be repudiated. You must be the Lord's entirely."[19]

4. *The place of regeneration.* The fourth costly error of the Dallas school is its failure to see the unbreakable link between justification and regeneration. The exponents of this view speak as if the only thing involved in the salvation of a sinner is justification. But Jesus also said, "You must be born again" (John 3:7). Clearly, there can be no justification without regeneration, just as there is no regeneration without justification. Regeneration means the creation of a new nature by God. In fact, it is only because Christians have been given a new nature that they believe in Jesus. Therefore, if one is justified, he or she is also regenerated, and if a person is regenerated, that person will have a new nature and will begin to act differently. The first evidences of the new nature are turning from sin in repentance and to Jesus Christ as Savior with true faith.

That is why I say that if there is no evidence of the new life, it is because there is no new life. And if there is no new life, the person is not a true Christian regardless of his or her profession.

TRUSTING JESUS CHRIST ALONE

To my mind, the best of all possible illustrations of true faith is the way a young man and a young women meet, fall in love, and get married. The first stages of their courtship correspond to the first element in faith, that is, knowledge or content. At this stage each is getting to know the other and is trying to determine whether the other person is one whose qualities would contribute to a good marriage. If they have any wisdom at all, they take considerable time to do this. *Is he the kind of person who would make a good husband? Is she the kind of woman who would make a good wife?*

The second stage is falling in love. It corresponds to the heart element, that is, to the point at which the other person begins to affect the lover in a personal and often emotional way. At this stage the man is not thinking about the woman abstractly: *Is this the kind of person who might make a good wife?* He is thinking: *That is the woman I want for my wife.* And she is thinking: *That is the man I want for my husband.*

Falling in love is a wonderful experience. But even that does not make a marriage. The marriage comes when the couple stands in church before their minister and recites the vows by which the two pledge themselves to each other. The man says: "I, John, take thee, Mary, to be my wedded wife; and I do promise and covenant, before God and these witnesses, to be thy loving and faithful husband: in plenty and in want, in joy and in sorrow, in sickness and in health, as long as we both shall live." She takes the vow too: "I, Mary, take thee, John, to be my wedded husband; and I do promise and covenant, before God and these witnesses, to be thy loving and faithful wife: in plenty and in want, in joy and in sorrow, in sickness and in health, as long as we both shall live."

This is how we become joined to Jesus Christ. Jesus died for us, demonstrating the nature of his true love and character. He wooed us, getting us to love him who first loved us. Now he takes the wedding vow, saying, "I, Jesus, take thee, [Susan or John or Mary or James, whatever your name may be], to be my wedded wife and disciple; and I do promise and covenant, before God the Father and these witnesses, to be thy loving and faithful Savior and bridegroom and Lord and God: in plenty and in want, in joy and in sorrow, in sickness and in health, for this life and for all eternity."

We look up into his face and repeat the words. "I, [put your own name here], take thee, Jesus, to be my loving Savior and bridegroom and Lord and God; and I do promise and covenant, before God the Father and these witnesses, to be thy loving and faithful follower and disciple: in plenty and in want, in joy and in sorrow, in sickness and in health, for this life and for all eternity."

Then God the Father, not an earthly minister, pronounces the marriage, and you become the Lord Jesus Christ's forever.

Yet there is a weak point to the illustration. In the case of a human marriage, both parties bring something to the new relationship. There is some measure of equality. But in the case of the divine marriage in which the Lord Jesus Christ purchases, woos, and commits himself to us, there is nothing that we have or can offer, and the bond flows solely from the unmerited grace of God in Christ, being made possible by Christ's work alone.

Here is how Paul writes about it in his own case in Philippians 3:4-7:

> If anyone else thinks he has reasons to put confidence in the flesh, I have more: circumcised on the eighth day, of the people of Israel, of the tribe of Benjamin, a Hebrew of Hebrews; in regard to the law, a Pharisee; as for zeal, persecuting the church; as for legalistic righteousness, faultless. But whatever was to my profit I now consider loss for the sake of Christ.

Paul is saying that, before he met Christ, he had something like a balance sheet in his life, a ledger showing assets and liabilities. He thought that being saved meant having more in the column of assets than in the column of liabilities, and since he had considerable assets he felt that he would do very well when he stood to give an account of himself before God.

He had inherited some of these assets. Among them were the facts that he had been born into a Jewish family and had been circumcised according to Jewish law on the eighth day of life. He was no proselyte, who had been circumcised later in life, nor an Ishmaelite, who was circumcised when he was thirteen years of age. He was also a pure-blooded Jew, having been born of two Jewish parents ("a Hebrew of Hebrews"). As an Israelite he was a member of God's covenant people. He was of the tribe of Benjamin.

Then there were assets he had earned for himself. He was a Pharisee, the strictest and most faithful of the Jewish religious orders. He was a zealous Pharisee, proved by his persecution of the church. As far as the law was concerned, Paul reckoned himself to be blameless, since he had kept the law in all its particulars so far as he had understood it.

These were important assets from a human point of view. But the day came when God revealed his righteousness to Paul in Jesus Christ. It was on the road to Damascus, where Paul was headed to arrest and execute Christians. Jesus appeared to Paul in his heavenly glory, and when he did, Paul discovered two important things. First, he understood for the very first time what real righteousness was. He had thought he was righteous. But now he understood that what he had been calling righteousness, his own righteousness, was not true righteousness at all but only filthy rags (Isa. 64:6). And he made another discovery too. He discovered that his own righteousness, achievements, or good works were not assets, as he had thought they were. They were actually liabilities, since by trusting in his own assets he had been kept from trusting Jesus Christ where alone true righteousness could be found.

So this is what Paul did: Mentally, he moved his long list of cherished assets from the column of assets to the column of liabilities—for that is what they really were—and under assets he wrote "Jesus Christ alone."

Augustus M. Toplady expressed the same truths in the hymn "Rock of Ages."

> Nothing in my hand I bring,
> Simply to Thy cross I cling;
> Naked, come to Thee for dress,
> Helpless, look to Thee for grace;
> Foul, I to the fountain fly,
> Wash me, Saviour, or I die! . . .
>
> Rock of Ages, cleft for me,
> Let me hide myself in Thee.

When those who have been made alive by God turn from attempts to establish and please God by their own righteousness, which can only condemn them, and instead embrace the Lord Jesus Christ alone, by faith alone, rejoicing in the grace of God alone, God declares their sins to have been atoned for by the death of his beloved Son, and he justifies them solely by his own perfect righteousness applied to their account. This is Christianity. This is the gospel, and to believe it and commit oneself to Jesus Christ is salvation.

John Calvin put it well when he wrote: "Let it therefore remain settled that this proposition is exclusive, that we are justified in no other way than by faith, or, which comes to the same thing, that we are justified by faith alone."[20]

SEVEN

Glory to God Alone

Creation, life, salvation too,
And all things else, both good and true,
Come from and through our God always,
And fill our hearts with grateful praise.
Come, lift your voice to heaven's high throne,
And glory give to God alone!

Before I became the pastor of Tenth Presbyterian Church in Philadelphia, I worked in Washington, D. C., for *Christianity Today*, and one of the games the newspeople at the magazine played in idle moments was "Whatever happened to . . . ?" One reporter would ask, "Whatever happened to Spiro Agnew?" Agnew had been vice president under Richard Nixon but had left politics after pleading no contest to tax evasion charges. The others would have to tell where he was and what he was doing at that moment. Whatever happened to Robert MacNamara, a former secretary of state? Whatever happened to Timothy Leary? Pierre Salinger? Huey Newton? These people had been in the news but had dropped out of sight, and the reporters' game was to keep track of them. Good reporters could keep track of people for years.

I was never very good at this game, which was one reason why I turned down an invitation to consider becoming editor of the magazine some years later.

This game cannot only be played with the names of people who have been in the news, however. It can also be played with theology. "Whatever became of sin?" asked Karl Menninger in a popular book some years ago, when he noticed that the awareness of sin was dropping out of contemporary life. "Whatever happened to Scripture alone? Christ alone? Grace alone? Faith alone?" are what I have been asking.

"Whatever happened to God?" is the question we need to ask in this chapter.

THE PROBLEM IN TODAY'S CHURCH

When he was only twenty years old, the great Baptist preacher and evangelist Charles Haddon Spurgeon began his half-century-long career in London with a sermon on knowing God in which he argued that "the proper study of God's elect is God." It was a remarkable sermon for a preacher who was only twenty years old. Spurgeon said, "The highest science, the loftiest speculation, the mightiest philosophy, which can ever engage the attention of a child of God, is the name, the nature, the person, the work, the doings, and the existence of the great God whom he calls his Father." He argued that thinking about God improves and expands the mind.[1]

But how many in our day regularly think about God, even in evangelical churches? It is impossible to know what is going on in another person's mind, of course. But judging by our actions, words, and church programs, I would suggest that not one in a hundred average churchgoers today actively thinks about God or stands in awe of him as part of an average Sunday service. Our minds are on ourselves. And even when we focus on the sermon, it is usually the case that we are directed to think about our needs rather than about God—who he is, what he has done, and what he requires of us.

Earlier in this century there was a wise Christian and Missionary Alliance pastor in Chicago named A. W. Tozer. He wrote a book on the attributes of God in which he explained how he saw the situation nearly forty years ago:

The church has surrendered her once lofty concept of God and has substituted for it one so low, so ignoble, as to be utterly unworthy of thinking, worshiping men. This she has done not deliberately, but little by little and without her knowledge; and her very unawareness only makes her situation all the more tragic. This low view of God entertained almost universally among Christians is the cause of a hundred lesser evils everywhere among us. A whole new philosophy of the Christian life has resulted from this one basic error in our religious thinking.

With our loss of the sense of majesty has come the further loss of religious awe and consciousness of the divine Presence. We have lost our spirit of worship and our ability to withdraw inwardly to meet God in adoring silence. Modern Christianity is simply not producing the kind of Christian who can appreciate or experience the life in the Spirit. The words, "Be still, and know that I am God," mean next to nothing to the self-confident, bustling worshiper in this middle period of the twentieth century.

This loss of the concept of majesty has come just when the forces of religion are making dramatic gains and the churches are more prosperous than at any time within the past several hundred years. But the alarming thing is that our gains are mostly external and our losses wholly internal; and since it is the *quality* of our religion that is affected by internal conditions, it may be that our supposed gains are but losses spread over a wider field.[2]

Who can suppose that the situation has improved over the last five decades? Clearly it has not. On the contrary, our escalating pre-occupation with television trivia and our growing addiction to the me-centered entertainment and worldly outlooks of our culture has made the situation worse. And the saddest thing is that most Christians are largely unaware of what has happened.

No people ever rise higher than their idea of God. Conversely, the loss of the sense of God's high and awesome character always leads to the loss of a people's highest ideals, moral values, and even what we commonly call humanity, not to mention the loss of

understanding of and appreciation for the most essential Bible doctrines. We are startled by the disregard for human life that has overtaken large segments of the United States. But what do we expect
to see when a country as proudly secular as ours openly turns its
back on God? We deplore the breakdown of moral standards in the
church, even among its most visible leaders. But what do we think
should happen when we have focused on ourselves and our own,
often trivial needs rather than on God, ignoring his holiness and
excusing our most blatant sins? To listen to many contemporary
sermons one would think that man's chief end is to glorify himself
and cruise the malls.

Tozer wrote, "What comes into our minds when we think
about God is the most important thing about us."[3] True. But if
the full truth be honestly told, many of us hardly think about
God at all.

Addressing this deplorable lack in the Cambridge Declaration,
the Alliance of Confessing Evangelicals viewed it as the ultimate
reason for the evangelical church's loss of Scripture alone, Christ
alone, grace alone, and faith alone. That is, it is not only the case
that a grasp of the first four *solas* leads naturally to *soli Deo gloria*,
as I said earlier; it is also the case that a loss of a concern for God's
glory undermines and eventually casts off the other *solas*. The
Cambridge Declaration recognizes this when it says:

> Whenever in the church biblical authority has been lost,
> Christ has been displaced, the gospel has been distorted, or
> faith has been perverted, it has always been for one reason:
> our interests have displaced God's and we are doing his
> work in our way. The loss of God's centrality in the life of
> today's church is common and lamentable. It is this loss that
> allows us to transform worship into entertainment, gospel
> preaching into marketing, believing into technique, being
> good into feeling good about ourselves, and faithfulness into
> being successful. As a result, God, Christ and the Bible have
> come to mean too little to us and rest too inconsequentially
> upon us.[4]

A CHRISTIAN WORLDVIEW TEXT

The apostle Paul thought about God and stood in awe of him, and there is no better example of his thoroughly God-centered world-view than Romans 11:36. It is what I call a "Christian worldview text." At the end of a doxology in which he is marveling at the unfathomable knowledge and wisdom of God, Paul declares, "For from him and through him and to him are all things. To him be the glory forever! Amen."

This text is remarkable for several reasons, and one of them is the position it occupies in Romans. The doxology comes at the end of chapter 11, after Paul has laid out the great theological sections of that book. He has explained our hopelessly lost condition due to sin, the work of Christ in rescuing us from God's wrath, the permanent nature of our salvation in Christ, and (in some ways most remarkable of all) what God is doing in world history—how he is using the rejection of Jesus by the Jews to bring the gospel to the Gentiles, and how he will yet work among the Jews as a people. This is remarkable theology. But when Paul gets to the end he does not glory in what he knows and has been able to explain to others, but in how little any of us actually understand God:

> Oh, the depth of the riches of the wisdom and knowledge of God!
> How unsearchable his judgments, and his paths beyond tracing out!
> "Who has known the mind of the Lord? Or who has been his counselor?"
> "Who has ever given to God, that God should repay him?"
> For from him and through him and to him are all things.
> To him be the glory forever! Amen (vv. 33-36).

Those last sentences are not the only verses in Paul's writings that are along these lines, of course. We might think of 1 Corinthians 8:6 ("There is but one God, the Father, from whom all things came and for whom we live; and there is but one Lord, Jesus Christ, through whom all things came and through whom we live"); or Ephesians 4:4, 6 ("There is . . . one God and Father of all, who is over all and through all and in all"); or Colossians 1:16 ("For by him all things were created: things in heaven and on earth, visible and invisible, whether thrones or powers or rulers or authorities; all things were created by him and for him"). Yet Romans 11:36 stands out from these other verses as a particularly succinct statement of the Christian outlook.

There are several areas in which we need to think about what this means:

1. *God and creation.* We think of the creation first because of the words "all things." All *things* includes the physical universe as well as intangible things such as truth, virtue, and the gospel. So, just as a starter, Romans 11:36 teaches that everything in the universe is from God, has come into existence and is sustained through God's creative power, and is for God's glory. John Murray unfolds the meaning of the verse like this: God "is the source of all things in that they have proceeded from him; he is the Creator. He is the agent through whom all things subsist and are directed to their proper end. And he is the last end to whose glory all things will redound."[5]

There was a time when God was alone. In that time before all time, when even space did not exist, God, the great "I Am," existed and was as perfect, glorious, and blessed in his eternal essence as he is now. Before there was a sun, the Triune God—Father, Son, and Holy Spirit—dwelt in light ineffable. Before there was an earth on which to rest it, the throne of God stood firm. If that great God, dwelling in perfect solitude, chose to create anything at all, whether the universe of which we are a part or any other possible universe, the conception of it and plans for it must have come from him, since there was no other being or power *from whom* they could have come.

But it is not only that the plan has come *from* God. The actualization of the plan was *through* him as well. That is, he is also the Creator of the universe. When God set out to create the heavens and earth, he did not call for help—since there were none to help him. He did not make use even of existing matter, for matter itself did not exist. God created everything out of nothing (*ex nihilo*). Genesis 1:1 is one of the most profound statements ever written, for it is based on the inescapable assumption that if anything exists, then God, the uncaused First Cause, must exist and be the Creator of it all.

The creation is from God and through God, then. But the most important thing is what comes next: It is *for God's glory* too. Why did God create the heavens and earth? What is the purpose of creation? We think of the universe as being made for us. But since God is a purposeful God and planned the universe for an altogether wise and noble purpose before any of us existed, even in his own mind, it is clear that he could not have taken as his purpose a creature that did not then exist. And that means that his motive must be found entirely in himself. Creation must be for his glory.

This is the point of one of the most important writings of Jonathan Edwards, the seventeenth-century New England preacher who is probably America's greatest theologian. It is called "The End for Which God Created the World."[6] Why did God create the world? And why did he create mankind to inhabit it? Edwards asked. It could not have been because of some need or inadequacy in himself, since there is no inadequacy in God. God cannot be improved. Nor could creation have been demanded by anything outside of God, because there was nothing outside of God before creation. No external power could have caused God to act, because there were no other powers. Only his own overflowing nature and delight in the revelation of his nature could have caused it. Because of who God is, God did not merely wish to *be* all-powerful, holy, faithful, and true, concluded Edwards. God wanted to exhibit these qualities, so he created the world to manifest his great glory.

The psalmist expressed this beautifully when he looked out upon the starry heavens and declared in nearly inexpressible wonder:

The heavens declare the glory of God;
    the skies proclaim the work of his hands.
Day after day they pour forth speech;
    night after night they display knowledge.
There is no speech or language
    where their voice is not heard (Ps. 19:1-3).

How different from the "religion" of Carl Sagan, who looked out on the same starry splendor and intoned, "The cosmos is all that is or ever was or ever will be."

If God created the universe to display his glory, he must have created us for the same great purpose, for we are part of the creation. Why did God create mankind? The Bible is filled with statements that God's glory is the ultimate reason for our creation. In Isaiah, God refers to "everyone who is called by my name, whom I created for my glory, whom I formed and made" (Isa. 43:7). Speaking of the final restoration of mankind later in the same book, Isaiah says that God will do it "for the display of his splendor" (Isa. 61:3). Similarly, God indicates that he is jealous of his glory: "For my own sake, for my own sake, I do this. How can I let myself be defamed? I will not yield my glory to another" (Isa. 48:11). The best expression of this truth may be in the well-known answer to the first question of the Westminster Shorter Catechism, "What is the chief end of man?" Answer: "Man's chief end is to glorify God and to enjoy him forever."

Against the shallow, self-centered culture in which we live, this radically biblical view offers hope by saying that there is something infinitely better than a preoccupation with our own personal gains and happiness. And it warns us that anything less than this radically biblical worldview is ultimately unsatisfying.

John Piper calls this outlook the "continental divide" in theology. "If you really believe this," he says, "all rivers of your thinking run toward God. If you do not, all rivers run toward man. Settling this issue is worth many nights of prayer and months of study."[7]

2. *God and the gospel.* The second area in which we need to think through the meaning of Romans 11:36 concerns the gospel. Like the first, this too is obvious—though in a different way. The first is obvious because "all things" clearly includes the whole of the physical creation. The second point is obvious because it is the gospel of salvation by God's grace that Paul has been writing about in Romans. In this context we cannot miss that salvation is also from God, through God, and for God's glory.

Salvation is *from* God, first, for he has planned it all. Who else could have planned it? No priest. No rabbi. No shaman. No guru. Only God could have planned a way of salvation that meets the austere requirements of his unyielding justice and yet also justifies sinners. Only God could have planned a salvation that is apart from human merit or good works—it is all of grace—and yet be able to transform those who are saved so that they achieve a level of righteousness and produce good works that surpass the righteousness and good works of those who are trying to be saved by them.

The accomplishment of our salvation was also *through* God, that is, through what Jesus Christ has done. Salvation is not achieved through anything you or I have done or can do. On the contrary, it is what we have done that is the problem, not the solution. As far as salvation goes, we can do nothing. We rightly sing:

> There was no other good enough
> To pay the price of sin;
> He only could unlock the door
> Of heaven and let us in.[8]

This is what the Protestant Reformers were expressing when they joined the word *sola* to the core doctrines of the faith, particularly those that deal with what they called the "material principle." *Sola* means "only" or "alone," and they used it to express their strong understanding that Scripture, the work of Christ, grace, and faith were all for God's glory.

When the Reformers wrote about *sola Scriptura* ("Scripture alone") their concern was with authority, as we saw in chapter 3. They meant that the Bible alone is our ultimate authority—not the pope, not the church, not the traditions of the church or church councils, still less personal intimations or subjective feelings. These other sources of authority are sometimes useful and may have a place, but Scripture alone is ultimate. Therefore, if any of these other authorities differ from Scripture, they are to be judged by the Bible and rejected, rather than it being the other way around. This was so important to the Reformers that they called it the "formal principle," meaning that it gives form or substance to everything else. It was their intention, in affirming this, to give glory to God alone.

When the Reformers spoke about *solus Christus* ("Christ alone") they were saying that salvation has been achieved for us by Jesus alone and that this has been accomplished entirely outside of us, apart from anything we have done or might do. His death on the Cross has made a perfect atonement for our sins; nothing we do can make or contribute to that atonement. Moreover, in salvation Christ's righteousness is applied to us by the Father, and this is the sole ground of our justification; our righteousness does not enter into our being made right before God in any way. Luther spoke of this as an "alien righteousness," that is, a righteousness entirely outside of ourselves. It is from Jesus only. When the Reformers spoke about Christ alone they did so in order to give glory to God alone.

The Reformers also spoke of *sola gratia* ("grace alone"). Here, as we have seen, they were insisting that sinners have no claim upon God, that God owes them nothing but punishment for their sins, and that, if he saves them in spite of their sins—which he does in the case of the elect—it is only because it pleases him to do so. They taught that salvation is by grace only. By affirming grace alone they were giving glory to God alone.

When the Reformers spoke about *sola fide* ("faith alone") they were concerned with the purity of the gospel, affirming that the believer is justified by God through faith entirely apart from any works he might do. Justification by faith alone became the chief doctrine of the Reformation. This too means that God alone is given the glory.

In other words, each of the other *solas* leads to the last and final *sola*, which is "to God alone be the glory," the final point of Romans 11:36, which concludes with the words: "to him be the glory forever! Amen." When we ask why that should be, the first part of the verse is the answer. It is because all things really are "from him and through him and to him."

Think it through again.

Think about *Scripture*. It is *from* God; he is its source, since the Bible is God's Word. It has come to us *through* God's agency, that is, by the Holy Spirit, through what we call *inspiration*. It will endure forever *to* God's glory. Jesus said, "Heaven and earth will pass away, but my words will never pass away" (Matt. 24:35).

Think about *Christ*. He is *from* God, because he is God. He became man by a virgin conception accomplished *by* the Holy Spirit, and he lives *for* God's glory. Jesus said of himself in reference to God the Father, "I have brought you glory on earth by completing the work you gave me to do" (John 17:4).

Grace too is *from* God. It is God's by definition. It comes to us *through* the work of God and is *for* God's glory.

So also with *faith!* The Bible says, "For it is by grace you have been saved, through faith—and this not from yourselves, it is the gift of God—not by works, so that no one can boast" (Eph. 2:8-9).

Clearly the plan of salvation is to *glorify God.* To be sure, it also achieves an eternity of blessing for those who are redeemed. We benefit immeasurably, far beyond our power to express it, and we will praise God for it forever. But if we understand what Paul has been writing about in Romans 9–11, particularly Romans 9, we know that our personal happiness is not God's chief purpose in ordering the plan of salvation as he has. We need only ask: Why are some chosen to be saved while others are passed over? Why are some rejected? The answer in Romans 9 is that the plan of salvation is for God's glory and that God is glorified in each case, in the case of those who are not saved as well as in the case of those who are. In the case of the elect, who are saved, the love, mercy, and grace of God are displayed in great abundance. In the case of the lost, the patience, power, and wrath of God are equally lifted up (Rom. 9:22-24).

We may not like this answer to why some are saved and others are passed over, but it is what the Word of God teaches. The reason we do not like it is probably that we are far more concerned about promoting ourselves and our own glory than about honoring God.

GIVE GOD THE GLORY

If the entire creation is "from" God, "through" God, and "to" God, and if the way of salvation is likewise "from him and through him and to him," then you, as a part of God's redeemed creation, are also "from him and through him and to him." In other words, you also exist for God's glory and must give it to him.

Start with your natural endowments. Where does that inquiring mind of yours come from? That winsome personality? That attractive appearance and gracious disposition? That smile? They come from God. They have been designed for you by God's sovereign decree and imparted to you by his working. They are for his glory, not for yours. The Corinthians were a particularly vain people, boasting of their superiority to other people. Paul called them arrogant. But he asked them, "Who makes you different from anyone else? What do you have that you did not receive? And if you did receive it, why do you boast as though you did not?" (1 Cor. 4:7). Glorify God by your talents.

The plan of salvation was conceived by God, accomplished through the life and death of Jesus Christ, and the ultimate goal of it is God's glory. If that is so, you should abandon the arrogant assumption that getting saved was your idea or that it was deserved or accomplished by you, even in part, or that it is meant to honor you. It is not for your honor, but for God's glory. The Bible says, "He saved us, not because of righteous things we had done, but because of his mercy" (Titus 3:5).

Have you had any longings after God? Do you want to pray? Do you find that you want to read God's Word and come to understand it better? Do you seek to worship God? If those things are true *of* you, they are not *from* you. In yourself you have no true aspirations after God. The apostle Paul told the Romans that in our unregenerated state "there is no one who understands, no one who seeks God" (Rom. 3:11). Holy desires come from a holy God, and are created in you only through the working of God's Spirit. They are for his glory. Therefore, glorify God by your spiritual aspirations. Praise God for them.

What about victory over temptation? We live in a world in which sin and evil bombard us constantly and in every conceivable way. We are attacked even by the powers of evil themselves. What keeps you from falling? What enables you to stand your ground against Satan's forces? It is God alone. The Bible says, "God is faithful; he will not let you be tempted beyond what you can bear. But when you are tempted, he will also provide a way out so that you can stand up under it" (1 Cor. 10:13). It is God alone who preserves you. Therefore, glorify God.

Think also about your work, particularly your work for God as a Christian. How can you achieve anything except through him? Even the ability to plan a secular project or the strength to dig a ditch comes from God. But if that is true of even secular efforts, how much more true must it be of Christian work. Spiritual work must be accomplished through God's Spirit. So it is not you or I who stir up a revival, build a church, or convert even a single soul. Rather, it is as we are blessed in the work by God that God by the power of his Holy Spirit converts and sanctifies those he chooses to call to faith.

Many people are looking for and praying for a reformation in our day. But the only way it will ever come is if true believers rediscover God and seek his glory. God is the source of and sustainer of all things. Therefore, our purpose is to give God glory. When we learn that and actually do it, genuine revival and true reformation may come.

HALDANE'S REVIVAL

In the last century there was a remarkable European revival that started in Geneva, Switzerland, under the leadership of a member of the Scottish aristocracy named Robert Haldane. James Haldane (1768–1851), his younger brother, was a captain with the British East India Company. Robert (1764–1842) was the owner of the family's estates in Perthshire. When Robert was converted, in the decade before 1800, he sold a major part of his lands and applied the proceeds to advancing the cause of Christ in Europe. James became an evangelist and later a pastor in Edinburgh, where he served for fifty-two years.

In 1815, Robert Haldane visited Geneva, where he hoped to advance Christian work. One day when he was in a park reading his Bible, he got into a discussion with some young men who turned out to be theology students. They hadn't the faintest understanding of the gospel. So Haldane invited them to his rooms twice a week for Bible study. They studied Romans, and the result of those studies was Haldane's great *Exposition of Romans*, which I regard as one of the best on that book.

All those students were converted and in time became evangelical leaders in Europe. One was J. H. Merle D'Aubigné, best known for his classic *History of the Reformation in the Sixteenth Century*, the first part of which we know as *The Life and Times of Martin Luther*.[9] Another was Louis Gaussen, author of *Theopneustia*, a book on the inspiration of the Bible. That book is still in use in French-speaking Christian schools. Frédéric Monod was a chief architect and founder of the Free Churches in France. Boniface became an important theologian. Csar Malan was another distinguished leader. These men were so influential that the work of which they became a part was known as Haldane's Revival. It extended widely, in time spreading to Holland, where it influenced even the great Abraham Kuyper, who became one of that country's most distinguished prime ministers.

What got through to these young men, lifting them out of the deadly liberalism of their day and transforming them into the powerful force they became? The answer: the very verse we are studying—Romans 11:36. In other words, it was a proper understanding of and a passion for God's glory.

This was Haldane's explanation. We know it because of a letter he wrote years later to explain what had happened. Monsieur Cheneviere, a pastor in the Swiss Reformed Church in Geneva and a professor of divinity at the University, had noticed the change in these young men and had written to Haldane to ask where it came from. Cheneviere was an Arminian, as were all the Geneva faculty. But Haldane wrote to him carefully to explain how appreciation of the greatness of God alone had produced these changes. The letter can be found in Haldane's commentary on Romans. Here is Haldane's explanation:

There was nothing brought under the consideration of the students of divinity who attended me at Geneva which appeared to contribute so effectually to overthrow their false system of religion, founded on philosophy and vain deceit, as the sublime view of the majesty of God presented in the four concluding verses of this part of the epistle: of him, and through him, and to him, are all things.

Here God is described as his own last end in everything that he does. Judging of God as such an one as themselves, they were at first startled at the idea that he must love himself supremely, infinitely more than the whole universe, and consequently must prefer his own glory to everything besides. But when they were reminded that God in reality is infinitely more amiable and more valuable than the whole creation and that consequently, if he views things as they really are, he must regard himself as infinitely worthy of being more valued and loved, they saw that this truth was incontrovertible.

Their attention was at the same time directed to numerous passages of Scripture, which assert that the manifestation of the glory of God is the great end of creation, that he has himself chiefly in view in all his works and dispensations, and that it is a purpose in which he requires that all his intelligent creatures should acquiesce, and seek and promote it as their first and paramount duty.[10]

Today many evangelical leaders in many different denominations and church circles are talking about our need for a new reformation. They are right to do so. Moreover, they are not only talking about it; they have been praying for it too. I have been doing so myself. We need a reformation desperately. But Haldane's testimony suggests that the reason we do not see revival today or experience a new reformation is that the glory of God in salvation, as well as in all other areas, has been largely forgotten by the contemporary church, and that we are not likely to experience revival or witness a new reformation until the truths that glorify God are rediscovered.

How can we expect a revival so long as we are taking God's glory to ourselves?

Is God in the business of glorifying us? How can we expect

God to move among us greatly again, as he did in the days of the Protestant Reformers, until the people of God can once more truthfully say, "To God alone be the glory"?

PEOPLE WHO CANNOT GIVE GOD GLORY

There are many people who cannot glorify God in this way—the vast majority of people, perhaps almost all people in our day. I am thinking mostly of unbelievers. But this is also the case with many Christians.

1.*Unbelievers.* The secular people of our day cannot glorify God because they are trying to glorify themselves. They are doing what Nebuchadnezzar was doing in the days of the prophet Daniel, as we saw in chapter 2. Nebuchadnezzar was on the roof of his palace. He looked out over the great city of Babylon with its magnificent hanging gardens and took personal credit for the splendor stretched out before him. "Is not this the great Babylon I have built as the royal residence," he said, "by my mighty power and for the glory of my majesty?" (Dan. 4:30).

Those words are probably the best single expression in all of literature of what we call secular humanism—a concise expression of that rebellious spirit that sets itself up against God. For when Nebuchadnezzar said, "Is not this the great Babylon *I* have built as the royal residence, *by* my mighty power and *for* the glory of my majesty?" he was claiming that the world he observed was *of* him, *by* him, and *for* his glory, the very opposite of what is expressed in Romans 11:36. He thought Babylon was "of" him, because it was his idea; he was the architect. It was "from" him, because he had the wealth and power to build it. Therefore, it was "for" his glory and his glory alone.

God's judgment on Nebuchadnezzar was terrible and swift: "The words were still on his lips when a voice came from heaven, 'This is what is decreed for you, King Nebuchadnezzar: Your royal authority has been taken from you. You will be driven away from people and will live with the wild animals; you will eat grass like cattle. Seven times will pass by for you until you acknowledge that the Most High is sovereign over the kingdoms of men and gives them to anyone he wishes'" (Dan. 4:31-32). God judged Nebuchadnezzar with insanity, and as the consequence of his insanity he was reduced to bestial behavior.

Sometimes when we think of God dispensing judgments, we think of him acting somewhat arbitrarily, as if he were merely going down a list of punishments to see what punishment he has left for some special sinner. "Let's see now," he might muse, "Nebuchadnezzar? What will it be? Not leprosy, not kidney stones, not paralysis, not goiter. Ah, here it is: *insanity*. That's what I'll use with Nebuchadnezzar." But this is not the way it happened. God is not arbitrary. He does not operate by going down a list of options. Everything God does is significant. So when God caused Nebuchadnezzar to be lowered from the pinnacle of human pride and glory to the baseness of insanity, it was God's way of saying that this is what happens to all who suppress the truth about God and take the glory of God for themselves. That path ends in a kind of moral insanity by which we declare what is good to be evil, and what is evil to be good.

But it is not only insanity that we see in the case of Nebuchadnezzar. We see bestial behavior, too. For God decreed that Nebuchadnezzar would "live with the wild animals [and] eat grass like cattle" (v. 32). Indeed, later on it is even worse. We are told that "he was driven away from people and ate grass like cattle. His body was drenched with the dew of heaven until his hair grew like the feathers of an eagle and his nails like the claws of a bird" (v. 33). It is a horrible picture. But is it merely a dramatic Old Testament way of saying what Paul says in Romans 1–2, namely, that if we will not have God, we will not become like God ("knowing good and evil," Gen. 3:5), but we will become like and live like animals?

I think of the contrast in Psalm 8; the psalm both begins and ends with the words: "O LORD, our Lord, how majestic is your name in all the earth" (vv. 1, 9), while the middle part talks about the created order. The beginning and ending of the psalm teach that everything begins and ends with God, rather than with man, and

that if we think clearly, we will agree with this. Then it describes
men and women particularly:

> When I consider your heavens,
>   the work of your fingers,
> the moon and the stars,
>   which you have set in place,
> what is man that you are mindful of him,
>   the son of man that you care for him?
> You made him a little lower than the heavenly beings
>   and crowned him with glory and honor.
> You made him ruler over the works of your hands;
>   you put everything under his feet:
> all flocks and herds,
>   and the beasts of the field (vv. 3-7).

These verses fix man at a very interesting place in the created order:
lower than the angels ("the heavenly beings") but higher than the
animals—somewhere between. This is what Thomas Aquinas saw
when he described man as a mediating being. He is like the angels
in that he has a soul. But he is like the beasts in that he has a body.
The angels have souls but not bodies, while the animals have bodies but not souls.

But here is the point: Although man is a mediating being, created to be somewhere between the angels and the animals, in Psalm
8 he is nevertheless described as being somewhat lower than the
angels rather than as being somewhat higher than the beasts. This
means that he is destined to look not downward to the beasts but
upward to the angels and beyond them to God, and so to become
increasingly like him. However, if we will not look up, if we put
ourselves in the place of God, as Nebuchadnezzar did and today's
secularism does, then we will inevitably look downward and so
become increasingly like and behave like the lower creatures. We
will become beast-like, which is exactly what is happening in our
society. People are acting like animals, or even worse.

The world thinks that it can do without God, that it can go its
way with barely a mention of him and without any thought of being

answerable to him at the last day. That is insanity if God is truly sovereign, and the result is a world of bestiality and violence. We need to see that the world about us, with all its glamour, which we admire so much even as Christians, is an insane, bestial world. We need to turn our backs on its values if we are to glorify God alone and take steps toward that new reformation that is so much needed in our time.

2. *Arminians.* A second category of people who cannot say "to God alone be glory" are Arminians. Unfortunately, they are the vast majority of those who call themselves evangelicals in our day, which is a major cause of the problems that beset the evangelical church. Arminians believe in grace. They want to glorify God. Indeed, they can and do say "to God be glory," but they cannot say "to God *alone* be glory," because they insist on mixing human will power or ability with the human response to gospel grace.

A well-taught Arminian knows that God will not have boasting in heaven. She or he knows that salvation is "not by works, so that no one can boast" (Eph. 2:9). But if what ultimately makes the difference between one person who is saved and another who is lost is the human ability to choose God—call it free will, faith, or whatever—then boasting is *not* excluded and *all* glory cannot honestly be given to God *alone.* If in heaven someone should ask an Arminian why he or she is there and another person, who has heard the gospel and rejected it, is not, the Arminian will have to say, "Well, I hate to say this in heaven, because we are supposed to be spending our time here glorifying and praising God, but since you ask, I have to reply that the reason I am here and that other person is not here is that I had faith, and he did not. I chose to believe. I, by my own power, received Jesus Christ as my Savior."

Our Arminian friend may almost choke to say that. But if he is honest and faithful to his Arminian theology, he will have to say it, and to that extent some of the glory that belongs of God alone will be taken from God and given to mere humans. A person who thinks along these lines does not understand the utterly pervasive and thoroughly enslaving nature of human sin.

Is it any wonder that we are not seeing a new reformation in our day? How can we hope to see it when we are focused on ourselves and when so many are in love with their own supposed spiritual abilities? In my judgment we will never have a new reformation, not even small but genuine revivals, until we recapture the God-glorifying truth of grace alone. We are far from that. Indeed, we are in danger of losing any kind of gospel at all because of our flight from truth into self-love and subjectivism.

3. *Calvinists.* But I need to add that even Reformed believers need to recapture this true gospel, since even those who insist most strongly on the doctrines of grace cannot give God glory if they are, above all, struggling to build their own kingdoms and further their own careers, as many are.

I am a Calvinist. But I testify that in my judgment even most Calvinists are not seeking the glory of God in all things. We say we are. We consider ourselves to be the chief, perhaps even the sole true heirs of the Reformation. But often what we are really interested in is increasing our own small spheres of influence. We too want to be prosperous and happy, just like the world. Or if we think of Christian work, our true goal is frequently our own personal success, defined primarily by loyalty to our own programs, churches, and denominations. We want our programs to prosper, and we want to get the credit for it. We will not see reformation until there is profound repentance for these sins and a radical readjustment of our desires, goals, and methodologies.

I believe that good times are ahead. I find many throughout the church, particularly young pastors, who are dissatisfied with the shallow consumerism of our times—our crass evangelical marketing of the gospel, our sad self-preoccupation—and who want to recover a gospel of substance whose end is the glory of Almighty God. I join with them. I rejoice with them and in them. But we have a long way to go to that end. Can we get there? Not by ourselves certainly. But God will lead us to those better days if we do actually repent of our sin and seek to make him truly preeminent in everything.

Part Three

THE SHAPE OF RENEWAL

EIGHT

❧

Reforming Our Worship

Praises be to God the Father
And to Jesus Christ, the Lamb;
Glory, honor, power, blessing—
Songs of angels joined by man:
"Holy, holy, holy, holy
Is our God, the great 'I AM.'"

Several years ago I was invited to take part in a worship service in Geneva, Switzerland, that was about an hour and a half long. Four English-speaking congregations had combined to hold this service, and it had been promoted as a time when the congregations could all worship together, which was good.

About half of the service was music led by a youthful worship team. They used overheads, and we sang choruses, most of them repeated three or more times. There was even one hymn. My part, the sermon, was about forty minutes long. The service was not bad, as services like this go. But what struck me about it was its lack of traditional worship elements, especially since it was on a Sunday morning and had been promoted as a united *worship* service. There was no invocation, no confession of sin, no pastoral prayer, and although there was a Scripture reading, it was there only because I had chosen it as the passage from which I was to teach later.

I say again: This was not a particularly bad service. But it was part of a contemporary trend which shows how far most churches have moved from an older, better worship style that was thoughtful and genuinely God-centered, as all true worship should be.

Of course, some services are much worse. The *Los Angeles Times Magazine* reported on a church in southern California that advertises its service as "God's Country Goodtime Hour" and promises "line dancing following worship." Their band is called the Honkytonk Angels, and the pastor takes part.[1] *The Wall Street Journal* described a church in America's Bible-belt that calls itself "The Fellowship of Excitement." It ran an advertisement for a Sunday evening service that read:

> *Circus*! See Barnum and Bailey bested as the magic of the big top circus comes to The Fellowship of Excitement! Clowns! Acrobats! Animals! Popcorn! What a great night!

The same church once had the pastoral staff put on a wrestling match during a Sunday service, having hired a professional wrestler to train them how to throw one another around the ring, pull hair, and kick shins without actually hurting one another.[2]

What are we to think of these sad trends? Whatever they are, they are not worship. How can they be if they have abandoned the use of Scripture, in which God speaks to us, and have eliminated prayer, in which we speak to God? True worship is praise of God for who he truly is and for what he has done, and if that is not the very center and heart of what we are doing, our so-called worship is not true worship at all.

A FORGOTTEN ACTIVITY

A number of years ago I came across a statement by John R. W. Stott that often comes to mind when I think about Christian worship. Stott said, "Christians believe that true worship is the highest and noblest activity of which man, by the grace of God, is capable."[3] I believe that is true. But it highlights what is probably the greatest shortcoming of the evangelical church today, and that is that for large segments of the church, indeed for the majority of churches, true worship is almost nonexistent.

A. W. Tozer saw the problem more than fifty years ago. In 1948 he wrote:

> Thanks to our splendid Bible societies and to other effective agencies for the dissemination of the Word, there are today many millions of people who hold "right opinions," probably more than ever before in the history of the church. Yet I wonder if there was ever a time when true spiritual worship was at a lower ebb. To great sections of the church the art of worship has been lost entirely, and in its place has come that strange and foreign thing called the "program." This word has been borrowed from the stage and applied with sad wisdom to the type of public service which now passes for worship among us.[4]

That was fifty years ago! The situation has become much worse since then. Today many do not even hold to "right opinions." Our churches are beset by multiple heresies. The "program" has become a "show," and many churches have abandoned real worship intentionally and altogether.

Churches might begin to improve on this sad situation by answering these three important questions: 1) What is worship? 2) Why do we see so little of true worship today? And 3) What can be done to recover true worship for our own spiritual health and the health of our churches?

A DEFINITION OF CHRISTIAN WORSHIP

It is not unusual to read in books dealing with worship that worship is hard to define. I do not find that actually to be the case. I think worship is easy to define. The problems—and there are many of them—are in different areas.

Let me begin with the word *worship* itself. If we had been living in England in the days of the formation of modern English, between the period of Geoffrey Chaucer and William Shakespeare, we would not have used the word "worship" at all. We would have said "worth-ship" and would have used the word to indicate the worth of notable persons such as our rulers. When we used it of God we would have meant that in worshiping God we were assigning to God his true worth. "Worth-ship" would refer to knowing and praising God as he has revealed himself to be by his creation and in the Scriptures.

Or, to approach this another way, we might have spoken—as we still do—of "glorifying" God. What does it mean to glorify God? In the early days of the Greek language, when Homer and Herodotus were writing, there was a Greek verb *doke*, from which the Greek noun *doxa*, meaning "glory," came. The verb meant "to appear" or "to seem," and the noun that came from it meant "an opinion," the way something appeared to an observer. From that meaning we have acquired the English words "orthodox" (meaning a straight or correct opinion), "heterodox" (meaning another or erroneous opinion), and "paradox" (meaning a contrary or conflicting opinion). One honors a ruler by holding and expressing good opinions about him.

In the beginning *doke* could be used for holding either a good or a bad opinion, but eventually it came to mean only having a good opinion about some person, and the noun, which kept pace with the verb, then came to mean the "praise" or "honor" due to such an illustrious individual. In this way kings were assumed to possess glory in special measure and were "glorified." Psalm 24 uses the word this way when it calls God the King of glory:

> Lift up your heads, O you gates;
>> lift them up, you ancient doors,
>>> that the King of glory may come in.
> Who is he, this King of glory?
>> The LORD Almighty—
>>> he is the King of glory (vv. 9-10).

At this point we can discern the effect of taking the word over into the Bible and applying it to God. If a person has a right opinion about God, the person can form a correct opinion about God's attributes and thus can praise or glorify God correctly.

Now let's go back to the word *worth*. This good Anglo-Saxon word might have been used to express the essence of "glory" in the English language had not the French word *gloire* predominated. *Glory* was the Norman word, and the Normans were the new nobility. So we speak of "glorifying God" rather than "worth-ifying him," though the idea of assigning worth to God remains in our word "worship." The ideas are the same. To glorify God is to acknowledge his worth-ship, which is what praising him also means. So, philologically speaking, the glory of God, the worship of God, and the praise of God are indistinguishable.

This means that *the first and most important thing to be said about true worship is that it is to honor God*. If what we call worship is not God-centered and God-honoring, it is not worship.

Yet *worship also has bearing on the worshiper*. It changes the person. This is the second most important thing to be said about worship. No one ever truly comes to know, honor, praise, or glorify God without being changed in the process. I think here of what is surely the best definition of worship. It is from the pen of a great former archbishop of Canterbury, William Temple:

> To worship is to quicken the conscience by the holiness of God, to feed the mind with the truth of God, to purge the imagination by the beauty of God, to open the heart to the love of God, to devote the will to the purpose of God.[5]

In that definition the attributes of God—holiness, truth, beauty, and love—and his wise purposes are foremost. But these, rightly known, acknowledged, and praised, impact the worshiper in five ways: 1) quickening the conscience, 2) feeding the mind, 3) purging the imagination, 4) opening the heart, and 5) devoting (committing) the will. Thus, in defining worship, Temple has also given us an excellent description of the true Christian life and has defined true godliness.

"MAC-WORSHIPERS"

Why do we see so little of this true worship today? John Armstrong, founder and president of Reformation and Revival Ministries, edits a journal called *Reformation and Revival Journal,* in which he calls what often passes for the worship of God today "Mac-Worship," meaning that worship has been made common, cheap, or trivial. What is the problem? Why is so little of the worship that characterized past great ages of the church seen among us? I think there are several reasons:

1. *Ours is a trivial age, and the church has been deeply affected by this pervasive triviality.* Ours is not an age for great thoughts or actions. We have no heroes. We have very few great writers. However, we do have movie stars whose careers we follow closely. The making of movies and their success or lack thereof becomes fodder for network news. Sports events command attention. For many, sports has become almost a national religion. Moreover, ours is a technological age, and increasingly the first objective of our popular technological culture is pervasive entertainment. People watch television constantly.

In recent years I have held seminars in various parts of the country on developing a Christian mind, out of which came my book *Mind Renewal in a Mindless Age,* based on Romans 12:1-2. In those seminars and in that book I suggest that the chief (though not the only) cause of today's mindlessness is television. I explored this at greater length in chapter 2 of this present volume.

Television is not a good teaching or informing medium, as most people suppose it is. It is actually a means of largely mindless entertainment. Because it is so pervasive—the average American household has the television on more than seven hours a day—it is molding us to think that the chief end of man is to buy things and be entertained. How can people whose minds are filled with the brainless babble of the afternoon talk shows or evening sitcoms have anything but trivial thoughts when they come to God's house on Sunday mornings—if, in fact, they have thoughts of God at all? How can they appreciate his holiness if their heads are full of the moral muck of the talk shows? They cannot. So all they can look for in church, if they look for anything, is something to make them feel good for a short time before they head back to the television culture.

2. *Ours is a self-absorbed, man-centered age, and the church has become sadly, even treasonously, self-centered.* I have defined worship as being concerned with God and his attributes. It is knowing, acknowledging, and praising God. But we cannot do that if all we are thinking about is ourselves.

We have seen something like a Copernican revolution in this area in our lifetimes. In times past—in Tozer's day, for instance—true worship may not have taken place very often. It may have been crowded out by the "program," as Tozer maintained. But worship was at least understood to be the praise of God and to be something worthy of being aimed at. Today we do not even aim at it, at least not much or in many places.

Kent Hughes is the senior pastor of the College Church in Wheaton, Illinois. He has written about this problem and seems to hit the nail exactly on the head when he says:

> The unspoken but increasingly common assumption of today's Christendom is that worship is primarily for *us*—to meet our needs. Such worship services are entertainment-focused, and the worshipers are uncommitted spectators who are silently grading the performance. From this perspective preaching becomes a homiletics of consensus—preaching to felt needs—man's conscious agenda instead of God's. Such preaching is always topical and never textual. Biblical information is minimized, and the sermons are short and full of stories. Anything and everything that is suspected of making the marginal attendee uncomfortable is removed from the service, whether it be a registration card or a "mere" creed. Taken to the nth degree, this philosophy instills a tragic self-centeredness. That is, everything is judged by how it affects man. This terribly corrupts one's theology.[6]

And worship too! Clearly, we cannot focus on God and his attributes, delighting in God and praising him for who he has revealed himself to be, if what we are really thinking about is ourselves, and if our only reason for coming to church is to have our needs attended to, whatever we may imagine them to be.

3. *Our age is oblivious to God, and the church is barely better, to judge from its so-called worship services.* The tragedy here is not that the majority of evangelical Christians in our time deny basic Bible doctrines—certainly not the existence and nature of God. We are not quite heretics, at least not consciously or intentionally. The problem is that, although we acknowledge Bible truths, those truths do not seem to make a difference. In the words of David Wells, they lie "weightless" upon us.

In recent years, I have noticed the decreasing presence, and in some cases the total absence, of service elements that have always been associated with God's worship.

Prayer. It is almost inconceivable to me that something called worship can be held without any significant prayer, but that is precisely what is happening. There is usually a short prayer at the beginning of the service, though even that is fading away. It is being replaced with a chummy greeting to make people feel welcome and at ease. Sometimes people are encouraged to turn around and shake hands with those who are next to them in the pews. Another prayer that is generally retained is the prayer for the offering. We can understand that, since we know that it takes the intervention of Almighty God to get self-centered people to give enough money to keep the church running. But longer prayers—pastoral prayers—are vanishing. Whatever happened to the *ACTS* acrostic in which *A* stands for adoration, *C* for confession of sin, *T* for thanksgiving, and *S* for supplication? There is no rehearsal of God's attributes or confession of sin against the shining, glorious background of God's holiness.

And what happens when Mary Jones is going to have an operation and the people know it and think she should be prayed for? Quite often prayers for people like that are tacked onto the offering prayer, because there is no other spot for them in the service. How can we say we are worshiping when we do not even pray?

The reading of the Word. The reading of any substantial portion of the Bible is also vanishing. In the Puritan age ministers regularly read one chapter of the Old Testament and one of the New. Bible students profit from Matthew Henry's six-volume commentary on the Bible. But we should not forget that the commentary was the product of Henry's Scripture readings, not his sermons. His congregation received those extensive comments on the Bible readings *in addition to* the sermon. But our Scripture readings are getting shorter and shorter, sometimes only two or three verses, if the Bible is even read at all. In many churches there is not even a text for the sermon. When I was growing up in an evangelical church I was taught that in the Bible God speaks to us and in prayer we speak to God. So what is going on in our churches if we neither pray nor read the Bible? Whatever it is, it is not worship.

The exposition of the Word. We have very little serious teaching of the Bible today, not to mention careful expositions. Instead, preachers try to be personable, to relate funny stories, to smile, above all to stay away from topics that might cause people to become unhappy with the preacher's church and leave it. One extremely popular television preacher will not mention sin, on the grounds that doing so makes people feel bad. He says that people feel badly enough about themselves already. Preachers speak to felt needs, not real needs, and this generally means telling people only what they most want to hear. Preachers want to be liked, popular, or entertaining. And, of course, successful!

Is success a proper, biblical goal for Christ's ministers? For servants of the one who instructed us to deny ourselves, take up our cross daily, and follow him (Luke 9:23)?

Confession of sin. Who confesses sin today—anywhere, not to mention in church as God's humble, repentant people bow before God and acknowledge that they have done those things they ought not to have done and have left undone those things that they ought to have done, and that there is no health in them? That used to be a necessary element in any genuinely Christian service. But it is not happening today because there is so little awareness of God. Instead of coming to church to admit our transgressions and seek forgiveness, we come to church to be told that we are really pretty nice people who do not need forgiveness. We are such busy people, in fact, that God should actually be pleased that we have taken time out of our busy schedules to come to church at all.

Hymns. One of the saddest features of contemporary worship is that the great hymns of the church are on the way out. They are not gone entirely, but they are going. And in their place have come trite jingles that have more in common with contemporary advertising ditties than with the psalms. The problem here is not so much the style of the music, though trite words fit best with trite tunes and harmonies. Rather the problem is with the content of the songs. The old hymns expressed the theology of the church in profound and perceptive ways and with winsome, memorable language. They lifted the worshiper's thoughts to God and gave him striking words by which to remember God's attributes. Today's songs reflect our shallow or nonexistent theology and do almost nothing to elevate one's thoughts about God.

Worst of all are songs that merely repeat a trite idea, word, or phrase over and over again. Songs like this are not worship, though they may give the churchgoer a religious feeling. They are mantras, which belong more in a gathering of New Agers than among God's worshiping people.

Not long ago I came across an excellent study of worship by a Lutheran woman, Marva J. Dawn. I bought it initially because I was struck by the title. It is called *Reaching Out without Dumbing Down.* I had thought it was about evangelism, but it is actually about worship, and its chief point is that much of what we call worship today is not worship at all but is instead a glorification of ourselves. This is particularly true of what we often call "praise" songs. Dawn gives this example:

> I will celebrate, sing unto the Lord.
> I will sing to God a new song. (repeat)
> I will praise God, I will sing to God a new song. (repeat)
>   Hallelujah, hallelujah, hallelujah, hallelujah.
>   I will sing to God a new song. (repeat)
> I will celebrate, sing unto the Lord.
> I will sing to God a new song. (repeat) (repeat all)

I have never heard that particular song, but it is a fair example of what we hear in many church services. The chorus seems to be praising God—it claims to be praising him—but that is the one thing it does not actually do. As Dawn points out, "The verbs say *I will*, but in this song I don't, because although God is mentioned as the recipient of my praise and singing, the song never says a single thing about or to God."[7]

What is the song about, then? If we look at it carefully, the answer is clear. With all the repeats, "I" is the subject twenty-eight times. Not God, but "I" myself. And not even myself along with other members of the covenant community, just "I." "With that kind of focus," says Dawn, "we might suppose that all the 'hallelu-jahs' are praising how good I am . . . at celebrating and singing."[8] What is this but narcissism, an absorption with ourselves which is only a pitiful, sad characteristic of our culture? If we are self-absorbed in our worship services, as we seem to be, it can only mean that we are worldly in our worship, and not spiritual as we ignorantly suppose.

The praise songs of the Psalter do not fall into this trap, which is one reason why they are such good models for our worship and why they should be used in worship more often than they are. Think of just the last five psalms, as an example. They are a kind of praise climax to the Psalter, showing us what it means to praise God.

Psalm 146 begins with the personal element ("I will praise the LORD all my life," v. 2), since praise must be personal. But then it invites all God's people to join in: "Do not put your trust in princes, in mortal men, who cannot save" (v. 3), "Blessed is he whose help is the God of Jacob, whose hope is in the LORD his God" (v. 5), and "The LORD reigns forever, your God, O Zion, for all generations" (v. 10). It praises God as the creator who cares for and upholds the oppressed, hungry, poor, and imprisoned, and who watches over the alien, the widow, and the orphan. It is the proper starting place for the collection.

Psalm 147 uses the pronoun "he," referring to God, fourteen times and "LORD" eight times, which is to say that it is about God rather than about ourselves. "I" does not occur even once, and "our" is used just twice. Psalm 147 gives us seven reasons to praise God: 1) his care of his people (vv. 2-3); 2) his care of even the least significant of things and people (vv. 4-6); 3) his care of the animal world (vv. 7-9); 4) his delight in the godly (vv. 10-11); 5) his provision for Jerusalem (vv. 12-14); 6) his rule over the entire creation (vv. 15-18); and, best of all, 7) his gift of the written Word (vv. 19-20). It concludes:

> He has revealed his word to Jacob,
>   his laws and decrees to Israel.
> He has done this for no other nation;
>   they do not know his laws (vv. 19-20).

Psalm 148 explains *where* God must be praised: from the heavens above (vv. 1-6) to the earth below (vv. 7-12). It calls on every creature and, indeed, all things imaginable to praise God: angels, sun, moon, stars, sea creatures, lightning, hail, snow, clouds, winds, mountains, hills, trees, wild animals, cattle, birds, kings, princes, rulers, young men and maidens, old men and children. It is a wonderful *tour de force*, concluding:

> Let them praise the name of the LORD,
>   for his name alone is exalted;
>   his splendor is above the earth and the heavens (v. 13).

Psalm 149 tells the "saints" of God to praise him with "a new song" (v. 1), and more than that, to serve him with "a double-edged sword in their hands," inflicting judgment on the nations (v. 6). Verses 6-9 are an Old Testament equivalent of the church's "Onward Christian Soldiers."

Psalm 150 answers four important questions. First: Where should we praise God? Answer: Everywhere, in heaven above and on earth beneath (v. 1). Second: Why should we praise God? Answer: Because of who God is and because of what God has done (v. 2). Third: How should we praise God? Answer: With everything we've got—with trumpets, harps, lyres, tambourines, dancing, strings, flutes, and cymbals (vv. 3-5). Fourth: Who should praise God? Answer: "everything that has breath," that is, everyone (v. 6). The conclusion is obvious: Therefore, praise God (v. 6). "Let everything that has breath praise the LORD. Praise the LORD." Each of these last five psalms both begins and ends with those words: "Praise the Lord" ("Hallelujah").

That is how worship should be done.

RECOVERING WORSHIP

A disaster such as the one that has overtaken the evangelical church in our day is not going to be cured overnight. But we can make a beginning, and one way to do that is to try to understand what Jesus himself taught about worship. Strikingly, Jesus did this in what we would call a foreign or alien context, meaning that he did not do it at the temple of Jerusalem where we might have expected a discussion on this subject to have taken place, but in Samaria, an alien land, in the vicinity of Jacob's well.

Jesus had been traveling north with his disciples, from the area of the Jordan in the south to Galilee, and had stopped at the well of Sychar while the twelve were sent into the city to buy food. While he was there a woman came down the hill to draw water and Jesus opened a conversation with her, asking for a drink. This provoked the woman's curiosity since Jews generally avoided talking to Samaritans. Then, as the discussion progressed, Jesus touched on her loose moral life, and the woman tried to change the topic by asking him a nonpersonal "religious" question.

"Sir," she said, "I can see that you are a prophet. Our fathers worshiped on this mountain, but you Jews claim that the place where we must worship is in Jerusalem" (John 4:20).

Jesus' answer is the classic biblical statement of what true worship is about: "Believe me, woman, a time is coming when you will worship the Father neither on this mountain nor in Jerusalem. You Samaritans worship what you do not know; we worship what we do know, for salvation is from the Jews. Yet a time is coming and has now come when the true worshipers will worship the Father in spirit and truth, for they are the kind of worshipers the Father seeks. God is spirit, and his worshipers must worship in spirit and in truth" (vv. 21-24).

There are several important teachings to be noted in these words.

1. *There is but one true God, and genuine worship must be of this true God and none other.* Worship of any other "god" is idolatry. This is the point of Jesus' saying that the Samaritans did not know who they were worshiping but that the Jews did, and that "salvation is from the Jews." It was a way of saying that the true God is the God who had revealed himself to Israel at Mount Sinai and who had established the only acceptable way of coming to him and worshiping him, which is what much of the Old Testament is about. Any other worship is invalid, because it is the worship of an imaginary god.

We need to think about this carefully today because we live in a relativistic age in which anyone's opinion about anything, especially his or her opinion about God, is thought to be as valid as any other. But that is patently impossible. If there is a God, which is basic to any discussion about worship, then God is what God is. That is, he is one thing and not another. So the vital question is not whether all opinions about God can be considered equally or at least partially true, but rather what the one true God is actually like. Who is he? What is his name? What has he shown himself to be? That is the only question worth discussing. We can listen to the views of others. But the Christian position is that the true God has made his being and power known through his creation; his character at Mount Sinai, where he gave the Law; his purposes in history by his dealings with the Jews; and his personality and the way of salvation through the life, death, and resurrection of Jesus Christ. These matters are laid out clearly, propositionally, and comprehensively in the Bible.

So that is the point at which we start. There is only one God, not many gods, and this one true God has revealed himself to us in Christ but also in part through the history of the people of Israel, which is why we can also say, as Jesus said, "Salvation is from the Jews." Mere opinions count for nothing.

2. *Today the only way this one true God can be worshiped is "in spirit and in truth."* Here Jesus was indicating a change in dispensations. Before, this worship was centered in the temple at Jerusalem. Every Jew was to make his way there three times annually for the festivals. What took place in the synagogues was more like a Bible school class than a worship service. But this was changing now that Christ had come. He was to fulfill everything the temple worship symbolized and anticipated happening. Therefore, in the future (until the end of the new age) worship would not take place by going to any specified location, either Jerusalem or Samaria, but would be in spirit and according to the truths of God's Word. Christianity had to be like this if it was to become a worldwide religion.

Worshiping God "in Spirit"

What does it mean to worship God "in spirit"? This is not a reference to the Holy Spirit, since the Greek does not have the definite article before the word. Jesus was speaking of *our* spirits, which the New International Version and most other modern versions indicate by printing "spirit" with a small s. Jesus was teaching that in the new age which he was inaugurating, the place for our worship would not matter, since a person would be able to worship "in [his or her] spirit"—which could be anywhere.

Many people associate worship with the body. They suppose they have worshiped if they have been in the right place doing the right things at the right time. For many that means occupying a pew on Sunday morning, perhaps singing hymns. For others it may mean lighting a candle, crossing oneself, or kneeling in an aisle. These things are not worship. They may be aids to worship. In some cases, they may also hinder it. But worship is something better and different. It goes beyond such actions.

Neither should worship be confused with feeling. This is a bit harder to pin down, because true worship will affect us, as I pointed out earlier. It may affect our emotions. At times tears will fill our eyes. But sadly, it is possible for tears to come and for there still to be no real worship simply because we have not come to a genuine awareness of God. We might be weeping only for ourselves. True worship occurs only when the spirit of a man or woman, which is akin to the divine nature (for "God is spirit," v. 24), actually meets with God and finds itself praising God for who he is.

William Barclay says it well:

> The true, the genuine worship is when man, through his spirit, attains to friendship and intimacy with God. True and genuine worship is not to come to a certain place; it is not to go through a certain ritual or liturgy; it is not even to bring certain gifts. True worship is when the spirit, the immortal and invisible part of man, speaks to and meets with God, who is immortal and invisible.[9]

What About Music?

We need to talk again about music. For the fact that worship must be an actual meeting with and adoration of God must have bearing on how we use music in our churches. This is a divisive subject, because music establishes emotional holds on people and we find it hard to give up anything with which we are "in love." Yet we need to think about the role of music carefully, if only because it is so engaging and influential. Can we use contemporary as well as traditional music? The answer is similar to deciding whether we will use extemporaneous or recited prayers: It *depends entirely on what these elements actually accomplish in the service.*

If the chief end of the service elements is to turn the attention of the worshiper away from himself (and even from the service itself) to God, then the first question we have to ask is whether this is what our music does. Does it direct our thoughts to God? Does it remind us of something about God and encourage us to praise him for being like this? Does it recall the great acts of God in our salvation and evoke a sense of gratitude for what God has done? Or, on the other hand, does it evoke merely an emotional, clap-happy feeling or euphoria? I am afraid that much of our music falls into this latter category, with the result that people leave our services having laughed and shouted and sung, saying, "Wasn't that a wonderful worship service?" when all they really mean is that they had a good time. They may not have had even one serious thought about God.

There is a second question we need to ask about our music, though it is harder to answer than the first question: What is the best music? And what are the best words? We are told in Philippians (where, as we have seen, Paul deliberately uses terms from secular Greek philosophy), "Whatever is true, whatever is noble, whatever is right, whatever is pure, whatever is lovely, whatever is admirable—if anything is excellent or praiseworthy—think about such things" (Phil. 4:8). That is a clear instruction to pursue the best in many categories. And if that is true generally, it is certainly true of music. We should use the best music we can find.

God is worthy of the best. We must not offer him blemished sacrifices. Part of a minister's responsibility is to point his congregation to the best in every area. Ministers should be lifting their people up to the best music as well as art, literature, and other things, rather than allowing them to slip downward to increasingly lower levels of the surrounding secular culture.

Sometimes we are told that music is merely a matter of taste. I heard that one summer from a pastor in whose church I had been speaking. I had been talking about a loss of absolutes in our culture and had mentioned the impact this has had on Christianity. I said something about the need for better music, and he challenged me by saying that "music is just a matter of taste." He had agreed with my teaching about the need to combat the world's relativism. So I pointed out that what he was saying was an example of that very thing. If there are absolutes, all music cannot be equally good. For in aesthetics, as in other areas, some music will be better than other music both in itself and for what we are trying to accomplish with it.

I am not saying that it is always easy to know what music is better. We need the help of our musicians here. But if we have nothing else to go on, one helpful test is whether a specific piece or style of music has withstood the test of time, just as we might ask what literature is best by determining which of the older authors are still cherished. Homer, Shakespeare, Dante, Milton, Dostoevsky, and others are literary examples. Examples in music might be Bach, Handel, or Mozart.

This also applies to the words we sing. The compositions of Martin Luther, James Montgomery, John and Charles Wesley, or Isaac Watts are clearly better than the repetitious babble of so many writers of today's ubiquitous praise choruses. Why should we commit ourselves so tenaciously to what is manifestly poor?

Worshiping God "in Truth"

The final thing we need to notice on the basis of Jesus' teaching of the Samaritan woman is that the true worship of God must also be "in truth." What does it mean to worship God in truth?

Here are several important things it should mean:

1. *We must approach God truthfully.* That is, we must come to him honestly. This is what Jesus was referring to when he said of the people of his day:

> Isaiah was right when he prophesied about you:
>
> "These people honor me with their lips,
>   but their hearts are far from me.
> They worship me in vain;
>   their teachings are but rules taught by men"
> (Matt. 15:7-9).

According to Jesus, there is no true worship unless there is honesty on the part of the worshiper. We must not pretend to worship. We must worship in truth, knowing that our hearts are open books before God.

2. *We must worship on the basis of the biblical revelation.* This is implied in the verses I just cited, for the verse which begins "they worship me in vain" goes on to condemn those who have substituted "rules taught by men" for Scripture. "Your word is truth," said Jesus (John 17:17). If we are to worship "in truth," our worship must be according to the doctrines of the Bible.

When the Reformation swept over Europe in the sixteenth century, there was an immediate elevation of the Word of God in

Protestant services. John Calvin particularly carried this out with thoroughness, ordering that the altars (long the center of the Latin mass) be removed from the churches and that a pulpit with a Bible on it be placed at the center of the building. This was not to be on one side of the room, but at the very center, where every line of the architecture would carry the gaze of the worshiper to the Book which alone contains the way of salvation and outlines the principles upon which the church of the living God is to be governed.

3. *We must come to God through Christ only.* That is, we must worship God "in Christ," with Jesus at the center of everything, for it is only in Christ that we can approach God at all or know who God actually is. Jesus taught this when he said, "I am the way and the truth and the life. No one comes to the Father except through me" (John 14:6). This is hard for people to accept. But it is for this very reason that God took such pains to teach it. It is what the instructions for the building of the tabernacle (and later the temple) are about. The tabernacle was not particularly beautiful, nor permanent. It was made only of pieces of wood and animal skins. Nevertheless, every part of it was meant to teach the way to God through the work of the Savior who would come.

The *altar* represented the Cross of Christ. It was given to teach that without the shedding of blood there is no remission of sins, and to direct the attention of the worshiper to the Lamb of God who would take away the sins of the world.

The *laver* was for cleansing, which Christ provides when we confess our sins and enter into fellowship with him.

The *table* that held *the bread of the Presence,* within the first enclosure of the tabernacle, spoke of Jesus as the bread of life.

The *altar of incense* symbolized prayer, for we grow by prayer as well as by feeding on Christ in Bible study.

Behind the altar of incense was *the great veil,* dividing the Holy Place from the Most Holy Place. It was torn in two when Christ died, to show that his death was the fulfillment of these figures and that today all God's people—not merely the high priest—may come to God directly through Christ's work.

Finally, within the Most Holy Place was the *ark of the covenant* with its *mercy seat*, upon which the high priest sprinkled the blood of a sacrifice once a year on the Day of Atonement. There, symbolized by the space above the mercy seat, was *the presence of God* to whom we can come by faith in Jesus, whose death paid the penalty for our sins.

Every element of the tabernacle pointed to how Jesus would open the way for us to God.

There is no other way to come to God. To come through Christ—the Christ of the altar, laver, bread of the Presence, incense, torn veil, and mercy seat—is to come in truth. We must come in that way only! However, when we do worship God "in truth," rather than according to our own corrupt inventions, we will find ourselves approaching again what the compilers of the Westminster Shorter Catechism rightly called the chief end of man. The catechism asks, "What is the chief end of man?" It answers, "Man's chief end is to glorify God, and to enjoy him forever."

John MacArthur, whose thoughts about non-worship we noted at the beginning of this chapter, explains what happened in his church when people began to take the nature of true worship seriously. "They began to look at superficialities as an affront to a holy God. They saw worship as a participant's activity, not a spectator sport. Many realized for the first time that worship is the church's ultimate priority—not public relations, not recreation and social activities, not boosting attendance figures, but worshiping God." And they were "drawn to the only reliable and sufficient worship manual," which is "Scripture."[10]

That is precisely what the evangelical church of our day needs most. And it is precisely what God wants from us.

Reforming Our Lives

God lifted me up to the heavenly realms
Where seated with Christ I am free;
In ages to come he will show me more grace—
So great is his kindness to me.
Yet now I am living with work to be done
For I am God's workmanship too—
Created in Christ with a race to be run,
Which God has ordained me to do.

Surveys of contemporary Christian beliefs and conduct tell us that most Christians do not act much differently from non-Christian people. This is not surprising, since little contemporary preaching teaches about or encourages a difference. But we should be very different, at least if we take the gospel seriously. Christians are to be the new humanity, a community of those who "love . . . God, even to the contempt of self" as opposed to those who "love . . . self, even to the contempt of God," which is how the great church theologian St. Augustine expressed it centuries ago in *The City of God*.[1]

How should we be different? The answer is: in all ways. In short, we need to recover what it is to "love the Lord your God with all your heart and with all your soul and with all your mind and with all your strength" and to "love your neighbor as yourself" (Mark 12:30, 31). Yet we also need a focus. I want to show in this closing chapter that the five areas in which the lives of today's Christians most need renewal are: 1) a fresh awareness of God's presence, 2) repentance, 3) an ordering of our lives by that which is invisible, 4) Christian community, and 5) Christian service.

Significantly, these things will be developed in us as we begin to recover and actually live by the essential gospel doctrines that I have been exploring in this book: *sola Scriptura* ("Scripture alone"), *solus Christus* ("Christ alone"), *sola gratia* ("grace alone"), *sola fide* ("faith alone"), and *soli Deo gloria* ("glory to God alone").

RECOVERING AN AWARENESS OF GOD

The point at which we need to start is with a renewed awareness of the reality and presence of God over against the preoccupation with man and his "felt needs" that has overwhelmed so many of our churches. There is a necessary balance, of course. Theology involves both God and man, just as good preaching must speak to both the head and the heart. But people tend to extremes, and the pendulum today has clearly swung in the direction of man-centered theology, worship, and church life. People come to church, if they do at all, with a "what's in it for me?" attitude, and the tendency has been to reorder the message and life of the church to answer that question.

David Wells has analyzed this tendency in several excellent books, including *God in the Wasteland: The Reality of Truth in a World of Fading Dreams,* where he writes:

> The fundamental problem in the evangelical world today is not inadequate technique, insufficient organization, or antiquated music. . . . The fundamental problem in the evangelical world today is that God rests too inconsequentially upon the church. His truth is too distant, his grace too ordinary, his judgment is too benign, his gospel too easy, and his Christ too common.[2]

In our day we obviously need to push the pendulum back in the direction of a concern for God and his attributes. We need to stress the doctrine of God again and again in our teaching.

But something else is needed too. Ever since Immanuel Kant attacked the objective distinction between the self and the object to be known by the senses, perceiving the mind actually to form reality by the way it receives and analyzes external stimuli, the self has become the measure and determiner of all things—for Christians as well as for nonbelievers. Preoccupation with self is the chief sin of the modern world. And this means that, without opposing the absorption with self, even a renewed effort to teach about God will be fruitless, since it will end only by presenting a God to be used by us rather than a God who demands from us a surrender of self and a radical obedience. We need to show that, in the Bible, God is not presented as an answer to our felt needs but as one who calls us to take up a cross daily and follow Jesus Christ.

Wells says, "In a culture filled with [religious consumers], restoring weight to God is going to involve much more than simply getting some doctrine straight; it's going to entail a complete reconstruction of the modern self-absorbed pastiche personality."[3]

We need to discover anew what it means to say *to God alone be the glory.*

1. *The sovereignty of God.* We can never exaggerate the importance of God's sovereignty, for God is the greatest of all realities, indeed, the very ground of reality, and sovereignty is the most important thing that can be said about him. The other attributes of God are also important. But if in our minds we ignore, distort, or deny God's sovereignty, meaning the absolute determination and rule by God of all his works and creatures, God will no longer be God for us. His decrees and acts will be determined by something else, either by mere human beings or by circumstances or by some other cosmic power, and these other things (or nothing) will be our actual God. In order to be sovereign, God must also be all-knowing, all-powerful, and absolutely free. If he were limited in any one of these areas, he would not be truly sovereign. Yet the sovereignty of God is greater than any one of these attributes.

Sovereignty is no mere philosophical dogma, devoid of practical value. It is the one doctrine that gives meaning and substance to all the other doctrines. It is, as Arthur W. Pink observed, "the foundation of Christian theology . . . the center of gravity in the system of Christian truth—the sun around which all the lesser orbs are grouped."[4]

Thus far most evangelical Christians would probably agree, though they might feel that the sovereignty of God is not a very practical focus for Christian teaching today. But what we must also stress is the corollary doctrine to God's sovereignty, namely, that if God is sovereign over all things, then we are not—not even over the affairs of our personal lives. We are not in a position to determine what our lives should be or even what our true needs are, and we are certainly not to suppose even for an instant that the world revolves around us.

2. *The holiness of God.* Sovereignty may be the most important of God's attributes, but if there is a possible rival to it, it is holiness. This is the attribute the Bible mentions most—not sovereignty or love, but holiness. "Who among the gods is like you, O LORD? Who is like you—majestic in holiness, awesome in glory, working wonders?" asked Moses (Ex. 15:11). When Isaiah had his vision of God, he heard the seraphs crying:

> "Holy, holy, holy is the LORD Almighty;
>   the whole earth is full of his glory" (Isa. 6:3).

In Revelation, the four living creatures likewise cry out:

> "Holy, holy, holy
> is the Lord God Almighty,
> who was, and is, and is to come" (Rev. 4:8).

So also the saints who have been victorious over the beast and his image. They sing the song of Moses and of the Lamb, crying: "Who will not fear you, O Lord, and bring glory to your name? For you alone are holy" (Rev. 15:4).

Emil Brunner wrote, "From the standpoint of revelation the first thing which has to be said about God is his sovereignty. But this first point is intimately connected with a second—so closely indeed that we might even ask whether it ought not to have come first: God is the holy one."[5]

Today, to paraphrase David Wells and the Cambridge Declaration, God's holiness rests lightly upon us. One reason is that the holiness of God is difficult to understand, and evangelicals along with others certainly do not understand it. It is not just a question of morality, as if all we are saying when we say that God is holy is that he is always right in what he does. Holiness is more a matter of God's transcendence, what makes him *ganz anders* ("totally other") as German theologians say. It involves majesty, the authority of sovereign power, stateliness or grandeur. It embraces the idea of God's majestic will, a will that is set upon proclaiming himself to be who he truly is: God alone, who will not allow his glory to be diminished by another.

Yet failing to understand what the holiness of God means is only one problem, and a lesser one at that. A greater problem is that the holiness of God is something of which human beings must stand in awe, and there is very little about which people today do stand in awe, least of all God. In our time everything is exposed. There are no mysteries, no surprises. Even the most intimate personal secrets are blurted out on television to entertain the masses. We contribute to this frivolity when we treat God as our celestial buddy who indulges us in the banalities of our day-to-day lives.

Perhaps the greatest cause of our neglect of God's holiness is that holiness is a standard against which human sin is exposed, and we do not like that. In Scripture, exposure to God always produces feelings of shame, guilt, embarrassment, and terror. Since these are painful emotions, we do everything possible to avoid them. One evidence of this is the way in contemporary culture that we have eliminated sin as a category for describing human actions. Karl Menninger, founder of the world-famous Menninger Clinic in Topeka, Kansas, asked *Whatever Became of Sin?*[6] and answered that by banishing God from our cultural landscape, we have changed sin into crime (because it is now no longer an offense against God, which is what sin is, but rather an offense against the state) and then have changed crime into symptoms. Sin is now something that is someone else's fault. It is caused by my environment, my parents, or my genes.

Menninger suggests that psychiatrists have compounded the problem by "neglecting the availability of help for some individuals whose sins are greater than their symptoms and whose burdens are greater than they can bear."[7] This is what evangelicals have done too. We too have bought into today's therapeutic culture so that we no longer call our many and manifold transgressions "sin." We no longer confront sin directly. We no longer call for repentance before God, but instead send our people to counselors to work through why they are acting in an "unhealthy" manner, to find "healing."

Wells claims that holiness defines the fundamental character of God and that "robbed of such a God, worship loses its awe, the truth of his Word loses its ability to compel, obedience loses its virtue, and the church loses its moral authority."[8] It is time for us to recover the Bible's insistence that God is utterly holy, and to explore what that must mean for our individual and corporate lives. We must rediscover those passages of the Bible in which people were exposed to God's awe-inspiring majesty and holiness. If nothing else, we need to recover the *law*, without which salvation and gospel grace lose their power and eventually even their meaning.

3. *The immanence of God.* The chief characteristic of the holiness of God is transcendence, that God is different from and infinitely above and beyond us. "Immanence" means that at the same time God is also profoundly present with us and in everything. Paul told the Athenians, "In him we live and move and have our being" (Acts 17:28).

Evangelicals probably believe this for the most part. But it is one thing to believe in God's immanence and quite another thing to practice it. One man who did so was Brother Lawrence, whose conversations and letters are collected in a book titled *The Practice of the Presence of God.*[9] Brother Lawrence lived in the seventeenth century. He was born in French Lorraine, served as a soldier, and was converted through seeing a tree in winter and reflecting on the fact that within a short time its foliage would be renewed by the love and power of God. His conversion led him to the monastery of the barefooted Carmelites in Paris in 1666, where he was assigned to the kitchen and put in charge of the utensils. At first he hated kitchen work. But he set himself so to walk in God's presence that he could worship God and serve others in the most humble circumstances. In time Lawrence came to worship God more in the kitchen than in the cathedral, praying, "Lord of all pots and pans and things . . . make me a saint by getting meals and washing up the dishes." He died at eighty years of age, full of love and honored by all who knew him.

That is what the immanence of God should mean practically, and it should be rediscovered by many who imagine that they are close to God because they can talk about him glibly when actually they know very little about him and are hardly conscious of his presence in daily life at all.

4. *The wisdom of God.* When we say that God is wise or all-wise we mean that he is omniscient, of course. God could not be all-wise unless he were all-knowing. But wisdom is more than mere knowledge, more even than total or perfect knowledge. A person can have a great deal of knowledge—we call it "head knowledge"—and not know what to do with it. He can know a great deal about a lot of things and still be a fool. And there is the matter of goodness too. Without goodness, wisdom is not wisdom. Rather it is what we call cunning. Wisdom consists in knowing what to do with the knowledge one has, and in the ability to direct that knowledge to the highest and most moral ends.

Charles Hodge wrote that God's wisdom is seen "in the selection of proper ends and of proper means for the accomplishment of those ends."[10]

J. I. Packer says the same thing but emphasizes goodness:

Wisdom is the power to see, and the inclination to choose, the best and highest goal, together with the surest means of attaining it. Wisdom is, in fact, the practical side of moral

> goodness. As such, it is found in its fullness only in God. He
> alone is naturally and entirely and invariably wise. . . .
> Wisdom, as the old theologians used to say, is his *essence,* just
> as power and truth and goodness are his *essence*—integral ele-
> ments, that is, in his character. . . . Omniscience governing
> omnipotence, infinite power ruled by infinite wisdom, is a
> biblical description of the divine character.[11]

We need to be amazed and humbled once again by God's wisdom,
and learn to trust it.

If we really believed that God is all-wise and if we really wanted
to be wise ourselves, we would seek God's wisdom in the Bible—
fervently and consistently. We would study to be wise. But we do
not really believe in God's wisdom. Martin Luther wrote rightly,
"We are accustomed to admit freely that God is more powerful than
we are, but not that he is wiser than we are. To be sure, we say that
he is; but when it comes to a showdown, we do not want to act on
what we say."[12]

RECOVERING REPENTANCE

If God is holy (among his other attributes) and if we actually come
face to face with him or get to know him, then the first thing we
are going to become aware of is that we are not holy. That will lead
us to repentance. We will be like the tax collector who showed that
he knew God and was actually praying to God by the fact that he
confessed his sin and sought mercy (Luke 18:13). Sadly, many of
us reveal that we do not know God very much by the fact that we
are largely unconscious of our sin and therefore obviously do not
repent of it and seek mercy. We assume that repentance is something we did in the past, when we first became Christians; we do
not think we need to be repentant now. But we do.

And we will—if we learn again what it means to say *by grace
alone.*

We need to remember Martin Luther and the "Ninety-five
Theses," generally thought of as the launching point of the
Protestant Reformation. The very first of Luther's theses read:

When our Lord and Master, Jesus Christ, said "repent," he meant
that the entire life of believers should be one of repentance.

Luther had been taught that repenting meant to "do penance,"
because the church's Latin Bible, the Vulgate, had wrongly translated "repent" in Matthew 4:17 as *poenitentiam agite,* meaning to
"do penance." But when Luther was set to work studying the Bible
by his spiritual father Johannes Staupitz, he discovered that this
was not what the Greek word meant at all. He saw that what Jesus
was calling for was not an act of penance but rather a radical redi-
rection of mind which would lead to a transformation of the repentant person's life. Later he would write to Staupitz, "I venture to say
they are wrong who make more of the act in Latin than of the
change of heart in Greek."[13]

1. *Words for repentance.* If repentance is as important as Luther
came to see it was, we should expect to find it spoken of extensively
in the Bible. And, of course, that is exactly what we do find. The
most important Old Testament word for repentance is *shub.* It
occurs hundreds of times in the Old Testament, over one hundred
times in the book of Jeremiah alone. It means to change the direction in which one's life has been moving, to turn away from something and turn back to something else. It can refer to apostasy, that
is, to a turning away *from God.* But mostly it refers to a person's
turning away from rebellion *against* God, *to* God. It means a complete about-face.

Sinclair Ferguson has written that in the Old Testament context, repentance involves two important things: 1) recognizing that
offenses have been committed against God and the covenant he has
made with his people, and 2) turning away from sin in view of the
gracious provisions which the Lord has made for us in his
covenant. "Repentance is created by a sense of who God is and
therefore by an awareness of the true character of sin. It is a God-
centered response, indeed the beginning of true God-centeredness.
Turning away from sin and turning back to God belong together."[14]

In the New Testament there are three verbs usually translated
"repent." The first is *epistrepho.* It means to turn back, and it is used

to describe conversion or returning to the Lord, as in the case of the Thessalonians, who turned *to* God *from* idols (1 Thess. 1:9). The second is *metamelomai*. It conveys the idea of regret. The third and chief word is *metanoeo*. It refers to a change of mind leading to a change of life and lifestyle.

The nature of New Testament repentance is illustrated in Jesus' parable of the Prodigal Son (Luke 15:11-32). The son was preoccupied with himself and the good life that he thought was his due. So he took his inheritance, turned his back on his father, and ended up in a "distant country." There his resources ran out, and he found himself caring for pigs while longing to eat what the pigs were eating. At this point he remembered his father and the bounty of his father's house, "came to his senses," and began the long journey home. The parable teaches that repentance is not merely regret about what one has done or the ruin one may have made of one's life. It is a change of mind issuing in a reversal that takes us back along the road of our sinful wanderings. It creates a completely different frame of mind. Ferguson says, "This lies on the surface of the New Testament's teaching. Regret there will be, but the heart of repentance is the lifelong moral and spiritual turnaround of our lives as we submit to the Lord."[15]

2. *Life characterized by repentance.* This is why Luther argued that "the entire life of believers should be one of repentance." We repent at the beginning of our Christian walk because repentance is a turning from sin to God. Jesus said, "Unless you repent, you . . . will all perish" (Luke 13:3, 5). Paul told the Athenians that "God . . . commands all people everywhere to repent" (Acts 17:30). But repenting is also something we need to do throughout life, since we will always be struggling with sin and needing to turn from it. Paul told the Romans, "Shall we go on sinning so that grace may increase? By no means! We died to sin; how can we live in it any longer?" (Rom. 6:1-2). Christians are to live by faith. But genuine faith cannot exist where there is no repentance. These are two sides of the same coin. Faith is turning *to* or trusting in Christ. Repentance is turning *from* sin.

Ferguson highlights three elements common to all biblical references to or examples of genuine repentance:

1. *A new attitude toward sin.* "This will inevitably be accompanied by a sense of shame and sorrow for our sin (Luke 15:18-19; Rom. 6:21)."[16] This is not the same thing as mere shame or sorrow. Judas "repented," according to Matthew 27:3 (KJV), but this was not repentance in the evangelical sense of the word, and the New International Version rightly renders this verse only as "Judas . . . was seized with remorse." By contrast, David's repentance, recorded in Psalm 51, was genuine because, although it was marked by shame, sorrow, and regret, it was also profoundly God-centered and directed toward living an entirely new and different life. David prayed, "Create in me a pure heart, O God, and renew a steadfast spirit within me" (Ps. 51:10). People who have taken this new attitude toward sin will strive to obey God's commands. Like Zacchaeus, they will care for the poor and will return to others what they have taken from them unjustly (Luke 19:8).

2. *A new attitude toward self.* "Repentance also . . . means dying to the old ways, crucifying the flesh,"[17] what older writers called *mortification*. Repentance like this is *radical*. It does not trifle with sin or coddle it. It is also *perpetual*. It involves an

> ongoing, dogged, persistent refusal to compromise with sin. The Christian is a new person in Christ, yet he is imperfectly renewed. He has died to sin and has been raised to new life. But this mortification and vivification continue throughout the whole course of his life on earth. We are no longer what we once were, but we are not yet what God calls us to become; and as long as that is the case we are called to an ongoing battle for holiness.[18]

3. *A new attitude toward God.* Finally, repentance also implies a changed attitude toward God. Ferguson says that there must be a

> new awareness of the holiness and justice of God, but there must also be a recognition of his amazing and abundant grace and mercy.

Repentance comes from a true view of God. If he should mark iniquities, none could stand; but there is forgiveness with him, that he may be feared (Ps. 130:3-4). Evangelical repentance, the inauguration and continuance of this life of godly fear, is always suffused with the promise and hope of forgiveness. That is why, for example, the repentance of the people of God in the days of Ezra was encouraged by the prospect, "there is still hope for Israel" (Ezra 10:2).[19]

Clearly, the people of God need to recapture a new sense of sin, coupled with a new awareness of God's grace and the need for radical and perpetual repentance, if we are to be renewed in our lives as God desires.

RECOVERING THE INVISIBLE

The third thing we need to recapture in our day is the reality and importance of those things that are invisible. God is invisible, of course. But that is not what I am writing about here. I am writing about all spiritual things, particularly the goals of the Christian life and labor and what God is accomplishing in the lives of Christians to get us to those goals.

This is what directed and motivated Paul, as he explains in 2 Corinthians 4. Although he faced fierce opposition to the gospel, and he and the other leaders of the church were wasting away under the constant obligations and pressures of the ministry, neither he nor those others were defeated or discouraged. It was because, as he says, "Our light and momentary troubles are achieving for us an eternal glory that far outweighs them all. So we fix our eyes not on what is seen, but on what is unseen. For what is seen is temporary, but what is unseen is eternal" (2 Cor. 4:17-18). Unseen things are seen by *faith alone*.

In many segments of the church today we have forgotten to focus on the things that are eternal. Too much attention is given to growing large congregations, increasing already enormous budgets, erecting ever more elaborate buildings, and gaining recognition from the world. Developing a work is not unimportant, though the way we approach many of these goals is harmful. But what is so often missing is giving sufficient attention to what ultimately matters, namely: God himself, truth, spiritual rebirth, holiness in church members, and glorifying God in our doctrine, worship, and church life.

Abraham is an example of those who lived by faith in God, having their eyes set on what is invisible rather than what can be seen. In Hebrews 11 he is brought forward as a hero of faith, one who "looked for a city with foundations," that is, God's city, rather than an earthly city with earthly foundations that will pass away. The first words about Abraham in Hebrews 11 say, "By faith Abraham, when called to go to a place he would later receive as his inheritance, obeyed and went, even though he did not know where he was going. By faith he made his home in the promised land like a stranger in a foreign country; he lived in tents, as did Isaac and Jacob, who were heirs with him of the same promise. For he was looking forward to the city with foundations, whose architect and builder is God" (Heb. 11:8-10).

The goal of growing churches and expanding budgets is to make a difference in the world. But I would suggest here, as I have elsewhere,[20] that it is only people who live with their eyes on what is unseen who will be able ultimately to make any real difference in the world. What was it that brought about the most significant social and political changes of our time? In November of 1989 the Berlin Wall came down and communism lost its hold on Eastern Europe. That was a watershed year. What caused it to happen? The secular media were blind to the cause, as they are to all things spiritual. But the reality, which they were incapable of seeing or reporting, is that the changes came about because of the faith and spiritual vitality of the people of Russia and Eastern Europe.

The changes began in Poland among the dock workers of the Solidarity movement led by Lech Walesa. They were Catholics, and their spiritual leader was Pope John Paul II, himself a Pole and a strong supporter of the people's aspirations. They took a united stand because they wanted more than personal safety and a comfortable life.

Religious faith also lay behind the changes in East Germany. The pastor of the St. Nicolai Church in Leipzig had been holding weekly meetings where the people prayed for change, and on October 9, 1989, on the anniversary of the founding of the Communist party in East Germany, the Communist leadership tried to preempt the pastor's meetings by busing party members to the church to fill the pews before the regular worshipers came. The pastor used the occasion to preach to them, while the people gathered outside, and his courage led them to demonstrate for freedom. Their numbers soon grew to seventy thousand as others joined in, and the army was placed on alert. Under normal circumstances the army would have attacked the demonstrators. But the protestors were crying, "Let them shoot; we will still march." The army did not attack. The protests spread to Berlin, where a million people gathered. The wall was torn down, and the government was toppled.[21]

Nicolae Ceausescu was the president of Romania. He said that apple trees would grow pears before the changes that had occurred in East Germany would come to Romania. Socialism was in no danger there. But by Christmas Day of that eventful year Ceausescu was dead and the government had been overthrown.

Josef Tson, founder and president of the Romanian Missionary Society, was in Romania just after the death of Ceausescu and reported the details of the story, explaining that the end began with the preaching of a Protestant pastor named Laslo Tokes in the city of Timisoara. The government feared the effect of Tokes's preaching and sent police to arrest him, but the members of the congregation surrounded Tokes, declaring that they were willing to die rather than let him be arrested by the state police. On December 16, just a few days before Christmas, hundreds and then thousands of people joined the parishioners and marched on the main square of the city. One was a twenty-four-year-old Baptist church worker named Daniel Garva. Night fell, and Garva got the idea of distributing candles to the ever-growing multitude. He lit his candle, then the others lit theirs. This transformed the protective strategy into a contagious demonstration and launched the revolution. The next day, when the army opened fire on the people, Garva was shot in the leg and the doctors had to amputate it. His pastor went to the hospital to offer comfort, but the young man told his pastor, "Don't be sorry for me. It is true I lost a leg, but I am happy. I lit the first light."

The Romanian people did not call the events of 1989 a revolution. They said, "Call it God's miracle." Their rallying cry as they faced the stern faces of the soldiers was "God lives! God lives!" Imagine that, from a formerly fiercely atheistic country! The people also shouted, "Freedom! Freedom! We do not mind that we die!"[22]

Willing to die? That is the only ultimately valid test of whether one is a materialist at heart, as many of us are, or whether we believe in things that are invisible, things greater and more important than mere houses and bank accounts and fast cars. The sixteenth-century Reformers had that grand perspective. It is what enabled them to stand, suffer, and even perish for the gospel. Martin Luther expressed their conviction in the fourth stanza of the great Reformation hymn "A Mighty Fortress":

> Let goods and kindred go,
> This mortal life also;
> The body they may kill:
> God's truth abideth still;
> His kingdom is forever.

Do we share that conviction today in our country? There have been some who are willing to die for things that are intangible. African-Americans (and others) who died for social justice during the Civil Rights movement of the 1960s are examples. Others have paid the price of their convictions by doing the right thing even when they have lost their jobs as a result. But today most of us no longer share a high standard of commitment and self-sacrifice.

Aleksandr Solzhenitsyn said of Americans, in a famous graduation speech at Harvard University more than twenty years ago, "Every citizen has been granted the desired freedom and material goods in such quantity and of such quality as to guarantee in theory the achievement of happiness, in the morally inferior sense which has come into being during [these last] decades. . . . So who should now renounce all this? Why and for what should one risk one's precious life in defense of common values?"[23]

If you want visible, worldly success and a comfortable life, there are ways to achieve it. Get a good job. Play the market wisely. As far as churches go, sociologists and growth specialists will explain how to build a large congregation or develop a thriving para-church ministry. If you want to raise money for a worthwhile cause, there are experts who can tell you how to do that also. Follow the right techniques, and the desired results will usually follow. But most things that have lasting value are not like that. God has promised to bless his Word so that it does not return to him void, and to bless those who set their minds and affections on him. But the success God is looking for is not necessarily what we seek, nor is his timetable necessarily ours.

Bringing people to Christ and building Christian character takes time. Forming godly families and nurturing spiritual giants does not happen overnight. The gourd that cast its protecting shadow over Jonah sprang up in an evening, but it had withered by the following morning (Jonah 4:6-7). We need to grow oak trees and move mountains.

RECOVERING COMMUNITY

A fourth area in which we need to seek renewal is for our churches to become true spiritual communities: "community" because it is only as a community that we can model relationships, and "spiritual" because what we want to model is the unique qualities of life that being Christian brings. The twentieth-century English poet T. S. Eliot raised the point when he asked, in "The Rock," what our cities are about:

> When the Stranger says, "What is the meaning of this city?
> Do you huddle close together because you love each other?"
> What will you answer? "We all dwell together
> To make money from each other?" or "This is a community"?[24]

The church of Jesus Christ can model community as no secular organization can—not businesses, not schools, not the centers of entertainment or social life, not government or city agencies—only the church! Because the church gets us outside of ourselves as those who together have been made into the one body of Jesus Christ, we can think about and care for others. Churches have an extraordinary opportunity for reaching people for Christ through their communities at a time when other forms of community have broken down. There is no better place than the fellowship of Christians for embracing those suffering from ruptured marriages, fractured homes, and other destroyed relationships.

Since the 1970s there have been two major changes in the way Americans look at other people and relate to them: 1) our present-day mechanized society treats people as things that have a function rather than as people with a purpose; and 2) we have become preoccupied with ourselves, rather than seeing ourselves in community with and existing to help other people.

In *The Greening of America* Charles Reich wrote sadly but accurately, "America is one vast, terrifying anti-community. . . . Modern living has obliterated place, locality, and neighborhood, and given us the anonymous separateness of our existence. The family, the most basic social system, has been ruthlessly stripped to its functional essentials. Friendship has been coated over with a layer of impenetrable artificiality as men strive to live roles designed for them. Protocol, competition, hostility, and fear have replaced the warmth of the circle of affection which might sustain man against a hostile universe."[25]

Christianity offers something different at this point. God said, "It is not good for the man to be alone" (Gen. 2:18). Jesus said, "I will build my church" (Matt. 16:18). Both of those statements concern relationships and show how necessary and desirable relationships are. In Acts 2 we are told how the early believers worked at this goal, devoting themselves to "the apostles' teaching and to *the fellowship,* to the breaking of bread and to prayer" (Acts 2:42, emphasis added).

Do we do this? Sometimes, perhaps, but we could do better.

Michael Scott Horton sees the good and the bad and has written perceptively:

> Our churches are one of the last bastions of community, and yet, they do not escape individualism. . . . Many of us drive to church, listen to the sermon, say "hello" to our circle of friends, and return home without ever having really experienced community. Earlier evangelicalism was so focused on corporate spirituality that communion was taken with a common cup. . . . We hear endless sermons on spiritual gifts and how the body of Christ is supposed to operate in concert. And yet, our services often are made up of the professionals (particularly the choir) who entertain us and the individual, separate believers who are entertained.[26]

What makes a community? A community holds together because of some higher allegiance or priority. Christians are the community of those who are formed by *Scripture alone* and who, because of that, know that they are all sinners saved by *grace alone* because of *Christ alone*. They are not wrapped up in themselves. Therefore, they love each other and are able to stand together and welcome all types of people and races to their fellowship. They have a commitment that goes—or should go—beyond mere individualism; and if they do, they inevitably model genuine community in church settings. Such communities provide an unsurpassed opportunity for reaching the unsaved world for Jesus Christ.

RECOVERING SERVICE

Christians not only care for other Christians, of course. We are also concerned for unbelieving people in the world around us, which means that we are called not only to win but also to serve others for Christ's sake. This is not a discretionary matter. We have already seen from Christ's parable of the sheep and the goats that the separation between the people of God and the world is made on the basis of whether they have or have not served others for Christ's sake. It is because the righteous have demonstrated their faith by feeding the hungry, giving drink to the thirsty, welcoming the stranger, clothing the naked, caring for the sick, and visiting those who are in prison that they are received into Christ's eternal kingdom (Matt. 25:31-46).

Protestants especially, because of our insistence on the doctrine of justification by faith alone apart from works, tend to overlook the importance of good works. We need to recover the importance of good works as the necessary and inevitable outcome of genuine conversion. True Christians must lead lives that are different from and better than those they led before they came to Christ. God expects it; indeed, he requires it (Eph. 2:10). And the world expects it too.

Two decades ago, George Gallup, Jr., president of the American Institute of Public Opinion, reported on the nation's religious life in an address entitled "Is America's Faith for Real?" His studies had shown that eighty-one percent of Americans considered themselves religious, ninety-five percent of Americans believed in God, seventy-one percent believed in life after death, eighty-four percent believed in heaven, an astonishing sixty-seven percent believed in hell. Large numbers believed in the Ten Commandments. Nearly every home had a Bible. Almost all prayed. Nearly half of all Americans could usually be found in church on Sunday morning. But Gallup also reported that: 1) only one person in five said that religion was the *most* influential factor in his or her life; 2) although most Americans wanted religious education of some sort for their children, religious faith ranked below many other traits parents would have liked to see developed; and 3) only one person in eight said that he or she would even consider sacrificing everything for God.

Something was clearly wrong, and Gallup got to the heart of the problem when his surveys revealed glaring ignorance of the Ten Commandments, even though we profess to believe in them; high levels of credulity; a lack of basic spiritual disciplines; and a strong anti-intellectual bias where religious matters are concerned. Americans want emotional experiences rather than sustained, rigorous thought and the challenge of applying biblical values to their personal and public lives.[27] What Gallup was uncovering was the gap between those whose religion is only a cultural facade and those who are true Christians.

But here is the interesting thing: Because those statistics seemed so contradictory, Gallup devised a scale to sort out those for whom religion really did seem to be important. They were the one in eight, or twelve-and-a-half percent, who really would consider sacrificing everything for their religious beliefs or for God. Gallup called them "the highly spiritually committed." He discovered that, unlike the others, these people were a "breed apart," different from the rest of the population in at least four key respects:

1. They are more satisfied with their lives—and far happier—than those who are less spiritually committed. Sixty-eight percent say they are "very happy," as compared with only thirty percent of those who are uncommitted.

2. Their families are stronger. The divorce rate among this group is far lower than among the less committed.

3. They tend to be more tolerant of persons of different races and religions than those who are less spiritually committed. And most striking of all,

4. They are far more involved in charitable activities than are their counterparts. A total of forty-six percent of the highly spiritually committed say they are presently working among the poor, the infirm, or the elderly, compared to thirty-six percent among the moderately committed, twenty-eight percent among the moderately uncommitted, and only twenty-two percent among the highly uncommitted.[28]

Gallup's figures tell us that genuine religion does make a difference in one's life, which is precisely what we need. There are times in history when it takes a thousand voices to be heard as one voice. But there are other times, like our own, when one voice can ring forth as a thousand. So let's get on with our calling, and let those who say they know God show they actually do—for his glory and for the good of all.

Notes

Foreword

1   James Montgomery Boice, ed., *Our Sovereign God* (Grand Rapids, Mich.: Baker, 1980), preface.

Preface

1   Os Guinness, *Dining with the Devil: The Megachurch Movement Flirts with Modernity* (Grand Rapids, Mich.: Baker, 1993), 38. The quotations are from *Publishers Weekly* (February 10, 1992), 42; and Jack Sims in Brad Edmondson, "Bringing in the Sheaves," *American Demographics* (August 1988), 57.

2   For more information, you may visit the website of the Alliance of Confessing Evangelicals at www.AllianceNet.org.

3   James Montgomery Boice, *What Makes a Church Evangelical?* (Wheaton, Ill.: Crossway, 1999).

4   James Montgomery Boice, *Mind Renewal in a Mindless Age: Preparing to Think and Act Biblically* (Grand Rapids, Mich.: Baker, 1993).

5   These hymns have been published as *Hymns for a Modern Reformation,* which may be ordered at www.AllianceNet.org. A recording of the hymns by the Westminster Brass and Tenth Church Choir is also available.

Chapter 1: The New Pragmatism

1   David F. Wells, *No Place for Truth* (Grand Rapids, Mich.: Eerdmans, 1993).

2   Michael Scott Horton, *Power Religion* (Chicago: Moody, 1992).

3   John F. MacArthur, *Ashamed of the Gospel* (Wheaton, Ill.: Crossway, 1993).

4   John H. Armstrong, ed., *The Coming Evangelical Crisis* (Chicago: Moody, 1996).

5   Dean M. Kelley, *Why Conservative Churches Are Growing* (New York: Harper & Row, 1972).

6   Cal Thomas and Ed Dobson, *Blinded by Might: Can the Religious Right Save America?* (Grand Rapids, Mich.: Zondervan, 1999), 23.

7   Ibid., 82.

8   Ibid., 189.

9   Allan Bloom, *The Closing of the American Mind* (New York: Simon and Schuster, 1987).

10 Gene E. Veith, "Postmodern Times: Facing a World of New Challenges and Opportunities," *Modern Reformation* (September–October 1995), 18, 19.

11 Ibid., 19.

12 The complete text of this document may be found on the website of the Alliance of Confessing Evangelicals: www.AllianceNet.org.

Chapter 2: The Pattern of This Age

1   R. C. Sproul, *Lifeviews: Understanding the Ideas that Shape Society Today* (Old Tappan, N. J.: Revell, 1986), 35, emphasis his.

2   Harry Blamires, *The Christian Mind: How Should a Christian Think?* (Ann Arbor, Mich.: Servant, 1963), 44.

3   *Humanist Manifestos I and II* (New York: Prometheus, 1973), 13.

4   Ibid., 16, 17.

5   Herbert Schlossberg, *Idols for Destruction* (Wheaton, Ill.: Crossway, 1990).

6   Allan Bloom, *The Closing of the American Mind* (New York: Simon and Schuster, 1987), 25.

7   *Time* (May 25, 1987), 14.

8   T. S. Eliot, *Collected Poems 1909–1962* (New York: Harcourt, Brace, 1963), 156.

9   William James, *Pragmatism, A New Name for Old Ways of Thinking* (New York: Meridian, 1955).

10 William James, *The Varieties of Religious Experience* (London: Longmans, Green, 1902).

11 Michael Scott Horton, *Made in America: The Shaping of Modern American Evangelicalism* (Grand Rapids, Mich.: Baker, 1991).

12 James, *Pragmatism,* 192.

13 Pat Robertson, *The Secret Kingdom: A Promise of Hope and Freedom in a World of Turmoil* (Nashville: Thomas Nelson, 1983), 59, 66, 67.

14 Horton, *Made in America,* 47.

15 See James Montgomery Boice, *Mind Renewal in a Mindless Age: Preparing to Think and Act Biblically* (Grand Rapids, Mich.: Baker, 1993), 83-95.

16 Kenneth A. Myers, *All God's Children and Blue Suede Shoes: Christians and Popular Culture* (Wheaton, Ill.: Crossway, 1989), 162-165.

17 Neil Postman, *Amusing Ourselves to Death: Public Discourse in the Age of Show Business* (New York: Penguin, 1986).

18 Douglas Jones and Douglas Wilson, *Angels in the Architecture: A Protestant Vision for Middle Earth* (Moscow, Idaho: Canon, 1998), 34.

19 Ibid., 28.

20 Robert Schuller, *Self-Esteem: The New Reformation* (Waco, Tex.: Word, 1982), 64.

21 Horton, *Made in America,* 61.

22 Ibid., 50, 51.

23 Postman, *Amusing Ourselves to Death,* 100.

24 Ibid., 116-117.

25 Ibid., 123.

Chapter 3: Scripture Alone

1   Donald Grey Barnhouse, "Isaiah 55:11," in *Holding Forth the Word: 1927–1952* (Manuscript Collection of Tenth Presbyterian Church).

2   Ibid.

3   The complete text of this document may be found on the Internet at www.reformed.org/documents/icbi.html.

4   See James Montgomery Boice, *Standing on the Rock: Upholding Biblical Authority in a Secular Age* (Grand Rapids, Mich.: Kregel, 1994), 161-178.

5   Ibid., 179-193.

6   Albert Schweitzer, *The Quest of the Historical Jesus* (Baltimore: Johns Hopkins University Press, 1998).

7   James B. Pritchard, *Ancient Near Eastern Texts Relating to the Old Testament* (Princeton, N.J.: Princeton University Press, 1950).

8   *Time* (December 30, 1974), 41.

9   *Time* (January 13, 1975), 65.

10 W. A. Criswell, "What Happens When I Preach the Bible as Literally True," in Earl D. Radmacher, ed., *Can We Trust the Bible?* (Wheaton, Ill.: Tyndale, 1979), 91-108.

11 Marcellus Kik, *Church and State: The Story of Two Kingdoms* (New York: Thomas Nelson, 1963), 83. See 71-85.

Chapter 4: Christ Alone

1   The complete text of this document may be found on the website of the Alliance of Confessing Evangelicals: www.AllianceNet.org.

2   Emil Brunner, *The Mediator,* trans. Olive Wyon (Philadelphia: Westminster, 1947), 435. Original edition 1927. The Luther quote is from the standard *Collected Works* in German, vol. 25, 330.

3   Anselm of Canterbury, "Why God Became Man," in *A Scholastic Miscellany: Anselm to Ockham,* ed. and trans. Eugene R. Fairweather, "The Library of Christian Classics," vol. 10 (Philadelphia: Westminster, 1956), 119, 121, 122.

4   Brunner, *The Mediator,* 447.

5   Anselm, "Why God Became Man," 138.

6   Ibid., 176.

7   Martin Luther, *What Luther Says: An Anthology,* comp. Ewald M. Plass (Saint Louis: Concordia, 1959), vol. 3, 1423.

8   William Neil, *Apostle Extraordinary* (London: Religious Education Press, 1965), 89, 90. He is quoted in John R. W. Stott, *The Cross of Christ* (Downers Grove, Ill.: InterVarsity, 1986), 172, 173.

9   John Murray, *The Epistle to the Romans* (Grand Rapids, Mich.: Eerdmans, 1968), 116, 117.

10 Stott, *The Cross of Christ,* 173, 174.

11 Brunner, *The Mediator,* 524.

12 Ibid., 524, 525.

13 Horatio G. Spafford, "It Is Well with My Soul," in *The Trinity Hymnal* (Atlanta: Great Commission Publications, 1998), 691.

14 Nikolaus Ludwig von Zinzendorf, "Jesus, Thy Blood and Righteousness," in *The Trinity Hymnal,* 520.

15 H. E. Guillebaud, *Why the Cross?* (Chicago: InterVarsity Christian Fellowship, 1947), 130, 135.

16   J. I. Packer, *Knowing God* (Downers Grove, Ill.: InterVarsity, 1973), 51.

17   Isaac Watts, "When I Survey the Wondrous Cross," in *The Trinity Hymnal,* 252.

Chapter 5: Grace Alone

1   The complete text of this document may be found on the website of the Alliance of Confessing Evangelicals: www.AllianceNet.org.

2   J. I. Packer, *Knowing God* (Downers Grove, Ill.: InterVarsity, 1973), 117.

3   Ibid., 117-119.

4   Alexander Maclaren, *Expositions of Holy Scripture,* vol. 3, *The Psalms, Isaiah 1–48* (Grand Rapids, Mich.: Eerdmans, 1959), part 2, 5.

5   Jonathan Edwards, "A Careful and Strict Inquiry into the Prevailing Notions of the Freedom of the Will," *The Works of Jonathan Edwards,* vol. 1, revised by Edward Hickman with a memoir by Sereno E. Dwight (Edinburgh: Banner of Truth Trust, 1976), 3-93.

6   Packer, *Knowing God,* 117-120.

7   Charles Wesley, "And Can It Be That I Should Gain," in *The Trinity Hymnal* (Atlanta: Great Commissions Publications, 1998), 455.

8   Francis Scott Key, "Lord, with Glowing Heart I'd Praise Thee," 1823.

9   Samuel Davies, "Great God of Wonders," in *The Trinity Hymnal* (Philadelphia: Great Commission Publications, 1961), 71.

10   William Cowper, "God Moves in a Mysterious Way," in *The Trinity Hymnal,* 128.

Chapter 6: Faith Alone

1   John Calvin, *Institutes of the Christian Religion,* ed. John T. McNeill, trans. Ford Lewis Battles (Philadelphia: Westminster, 1960), 726.

2   Thomas Cranmer, "Sermon on Salvation" in *First Book of Homilies* (London: Society for the Propagation of Christian Knowledge, 1914), 25, 26. Original edition 1547.

3   Thomas Watson, *A Body of Divinity* (London: The Banner of Truth Trust, 1970), 226. Original edition 1692.

4   Martin Luther, *What Luther Says: An Anthology,* comp. Ewald M. Plass (Saint Louis: Concordia, 1959), vol. 2, 702-704, 715.

5   Leon Morris, *The Apostolic Preaching of the Cross* (Grand Rapids, Mich.: Eerdmans, 1971), 271.

6   J. H. Merle D'Aubigné, *The Life and Times of Martin Luther,* trans. H. White (Chicago: Moody, 1958), 31.

7   Ibid., 32.

8   John R. W. Stott, *The Cross of Christ* (Downers Grove, Ill.: InterVarsity, 1986), 189-192.

9   Charles Haddon Spurgeon, *All of Grace* (Chicago: Moody, n.d.), 27, 29.

10   R. C. Sproul, *Faith Alone: The Evangelical Doctrine of Justification* (Grand Rapids, Mich.: Baker, 1995), 77.

11   Calvin, *Institutes of the Christian Religion,* 542, 544, 545.

12 John Wesley, *The Works of John Wesley*, vol. 1, *Journal from October 14, 1735, to November 29, 1845* (Grand Rapids, Mich.: Zondervan, n.d.), 103.

13 Calvin, *Institutes of the Christian Religion*, 583.

14 Zane C. Hodges, *The Gospel Under Siege* (Dallas: Rendencion Viva, 1992); *Absolutely Free!* (Grand Rapids, Mich.: Zondervan, 1989).

15 John F. MacArthur, *The Gospel According to Jesus* (Grand Rapids, Mich.: Zondervan, 1994).

16 Charles Caldwell Ryrie, *Balancing the Christian Life* (Chicago: Moody, 1969), 170.

17 Ibid.

18 G. Michael Cocoris, *Lordship Salvation: Is It Biblical?* (Dallas: Rendencion Viva, 1983), 12.

19 James Montgomery Boice, *Christ's Call to Discipleship* (Chicago: Moody, 1986), 114.

20 John Calvin, *The Epistles of Paul the Apostle to the Galatians, Ephesians, Philippians and Colossians*, ed. David W. Torrance and Thomas F. Torrance, trans. T. H. L. Parker (Edinburgh: Oliver and Boyd; and Grand Rapids, Mich.: Eerdmans, 1965), 39.

Chapter 7: Glory to God Alone

1 Charles Haddon Spurgeon, "The Immutability of God" (Malachi 3:6) in *The New Park Street Pulpit* (Pasadena, Tex.: Pilgrim, 1975), 1. Original edition 1855.

2 A. W. Tozer, *The Knowledge of the Holy* (New York: Harper & Row, 1961), 6-7.

3 Ibid., 9.

4 The complete text of this document may be found on the website of the Alliance of Confessing Evangelicals: www.AllianceNet.org.

5 John Murray, *The Epistle to the Romans* (Grand Rapids, Mich.: Eerdmans, 1968), vol. 2, 107, 108.

6 The most accessible modern edition of Edwards's essay is in John Piper, *God's Passion for His Glory: Living the Vision of Jonathan Edwards. With the Complete Text of "The End for Which God Created the World"* (Wheaton, Ill.: Crossway, 1998).

7 Piper, *God's Passion for His Glory*, 141.

8 Cecil Frances Alexander, "There Is a Green Hill Far Away," in *The Trinity Hymnal* (Atlanta: Great Commission Publications, 1997), 256.

9 J. H. Merle D'Aubigné, *The Life and Times of Martin Luther*, trans. H. White (Chicago: Moody, 1958).

10 Robert Haldane, *An Exposition of the Epistle to the Romans* (MacDill AFB: MacDonald, 1958), 552.

Chapter 8: Reforming Our Worship

1 Judy Raphael, "God and Country," *Los Angeles Times Magazine* (Nov. 6, 1994), 14; quoted by John F. MacArthur, "How Shall We Then Worship?" in John H. Armstrong, ed., *The Coming Evangelical Crisis* (Chicago: Moody, 1996), 175.

2 E. Gustav Niebuhr, "Mighty Fortress Megachurches Strive to Be All Things to All Parishioners," *The Wall Street Journal* (May 13, 1991), A6; quoted by John F. MacArthur, "How Shall We Then Worship?" 176.

3   John R. W. Stott, *Christ the Controversialist: A Study in Some Essentials of Evangelical Religion* (London: Tyndale Press, 1970), 160.

4   A. W. Tozer, *The Pursuit of God* (Harrisburg: Christian Publications, 1948), 9.

5   William Temple, *The Hope of a New World,* 30. Cited by Donald P. Hustad, *Jubilate! Church Music in the Evangelical Tradition* (Carol Stream, Ill.: Hope, 1981), 78.

6   R. Kent Hughes, *Disciplines of a Godly Man* (Wheaton, Ill.: Crossway, 1991), 106.

7   Marva J. Dawn, *Reaching Out without Dumbing Down: A Theology of Worship for the Turn-of-the-Century Culture* (Grand Rapids, Mich.: Eerdmans, 1995), 108.

8   Ibid.

9   William Barclay, *The Gospel of John,* vol. 1 (Philadelphia: Westminster, 1958), 154.

10 John F. MacArthur, "How Shall We Then Worship?" in John H. Armstrong, ed., *The Coming Evangelical Crisis,* 177.

Chapter 9: Reforming Our Lives

1   Saint Augustine, *The City of God,* in *A Select Library of the Nicene and Post-Nicene Fathers of the Christian Church,* ed. Philip Schaff, vol. 2 (Grand Rapids, Mich.: Eerdmans, 1977), 282, 283.

2   David F. Wells, *God in the Wasteland: The Reality of Truth in a World of Fading Dreams* (Grand Rapids, Mich.: Eerdmans; and Leicester, England: InterVarsity, 1994), 30.

3   Ibid., 115.

4   Arthur W. Pink, *The Sovereignty of God* (Grand Rapids, Mich.: Baker, 1969), 263.

5   Emil Brunner, *The Christian Doctrine of God,* vol. 1, trans. Olive Wyon (Philadelphia: Westminster, 1950), 157.

6   Karl Menninger, *Whatever Became of Sin?* (New York: Bantam, 1978).

7   Ibid., flyleaf.

8   Wells, *God in the Wasteland,* 136.

9   Brother Lawrence, *The Practice of the Presence of God,* ed. Harold J. Chadwick (North Brunswick, N.J.: Bridge-Logos, 2000).

10 Charles Hodge, *Systematic Theology,* vol. 1 (London: James Clarke, 1960), 401.

11 J. I. Packer, *Knowing God* (Downers Grove, Ill.: InterVarsity, 1973), 80, 81.

12 Martin Luther, *What Luther Says: An Anthology,* comp. Ewald M. Plass (Saint Louis: Concordia, 1959), vol. 3, 1453.

13 Quoted in Roland Bainton, *Here I Stand,* (Nashville: Abingdon, 1978), 67.

14 Sinclair B. Ferguson, *The Grace of Repentance* (Wheaton, Ill.: Crossway, 2000), 13.

15 Ibid., 16.

16 Ibid., 18.

17 Ibid., 19.

18 Ibid., 20.

19 Ibid.

20 See James Montgomery Boice, *Mind Renewal in a Mindless Age: Preparing to Think and Act Biblically* (Grand Rapids, Mich.: Baker, 1993), 106-108.

21 The neglected story of the role of the church in the changes that have come to Eastern Europe is told in part in, "How the East Was Won: Reports on the Rebirth of Christianity under Communism," *National Review* (January 22, 1990), 22-28.

22 From *Voice of Truth* (Romanian Missionary Society) (January–February 1990), 2.

23 Aleksandr Solzhenitsyn, "A World Split Apart," the 1978 commencement address at Harvard University, *Harvard Gazette* (June 8, 1978), 17.

24 T. S. Eliot, *Collected Poems 1909–1962* (New York: Harcourt, Brace, 1963), 156.

25 Charles Reich, *The Greening of America: The Coming of a New Consciousness and the Rebirth of a Future* (New York: Bantam, 1971), 7.

26 Michael Scott Horton, *Made in America* (Grand Rapids, Mich.: Baker, 1991), 169.

27 George Gallup, Jr., "Is America's Faith for Real?" Princeton Theological Seminary *Alumni News,* vol. 22, no. 4 (Summer 1982), 15-17.

28 Ibid., 16.

General Index

Abraham, 54, 77, 78, 91, 103, 136, 162, 203
Absolutely Free! 142
ACTS, 178
Agnew, Spiro, 149
All God's Children and Blue Suede Shoes, 52, 53
Alliance of Confessing Evangelicals, 14, 19, 31, 36, 90, 108, 109, 129, 152
"Amazing Grace," 109
American Institute of Public Opinion, 209
Amusing Ourselves to Death, 53
Ancient Near Eastern Texts Relating to the Old Testament, 70
Angels in the Architecture, 55
Anselm of Canterbury, 93, 94, 95, 97
Aquinas, Thomas, 166
Arminianism, 162, 167
Arminius, Jacob, 115
Armstrong, John H., 20, 172, 190
Ashamed of the Gospel, 19
assensus (see biblical faith)
atonement, 25, 34, 89, 90, 93, 95-96, 98-99, 102, 105-106, 131, 134-135, 137, 158, 190
Augustine (Saint), 27, 70, 115, 191, 192

Babylon, 45, 164
Bach, 55, 188
Barclay, William, 186
Barna, George, 29
Barnhouse, Donald Grey, 67, 68
Barth, Karl, 102
Bathsheba, 136
Berlin Wall, 203
biblical faith, elements of
    assensus, 139-140
    fiducia, 140-141
    notitia, 138-139
Blamires, Harry, 44
Blinded by Might, 27, 28
Bloom, Allan, 29, 47
Boniface, 162
Book of Common Prayer, 130
Brunner, Emil, 89, 90, 94, 102, 195

Calvary Church, 27
Calvin, John, 56, 83, 84, 115, 130, 138, 139, 140, 148, 189
Calvinism/Calvinists, 84, 168
Cambridge Declaration, The, 31, 36, 88, 108, 152, 195
"Careful and Strict Inquiry into the Prevailing Notions of the Freedom of the Will, A," 115
"carnal" Christians, 143

Castle Church at Wittenberg, 38, 144
Ceausescu, Nicolae, 204
Chaucer, Geoffrey, 173
Cheneviere, Monsieur, 162
"Chicago Statement on Biblical Hermeneutics, The," 68
"Chicago Statement on Biblical Inerrancy, The," 68
"Chicago Statement on the Application of the Bible to Contemporary Issues, The," 68
church/churches
    affected by culture, 31, 54-59
    American, 24
    authority of, 34, 196
    contemporary life, 13-14, 163
    denominations, 21, 23, 114, 130, 163, 168
    fundamentalist, 42
    government of, 32
    growth, 13, 30, 50, 57
    liberal, 20-23
    mainline, 21-23
    medieval, 34, 36, 66, 107, 132, 138
    mega-, 55
    parachurch organizations, 31, 79, 206
Christ alone (see *solas*)
Christian Century, The, 20, 29, 71
Christianity Today, 20, 29, 149
Church of England, 130
City of God, The, 191, 192
Civil Rights movement, 205
Closing of the American Mind, The, 29, 47
CNN, 58
Cocoris, G. Michael, 143
College Church, 177
Coming Evangelical Crisis, The, 20, 172, 190
community, 181, 191-192, 206-208
confession, 110, 111, 141, 171, 178, 179-180
conversion, 75, 135, 136, 139, 144, 197, 200, 209
cosmos, 43, 48, 156
Council of Two Hundred, 83
Count Zinzendorf, 103
Cowper, William, 127
Cox, Harvey, 71
Cranmer, Thomas, 130
creation, 19, 104, 107, 122, 149, 154-156, 159-160, 163, 174, 182, 184
Criswell, W. A., 78, 79
Cross of Christ, The, 97, 98, 134
Crystal Cathedral, 56
Csar Malan, 162
Cur Deus Homo? 93

Dallas school, the, 143, 144

Scripture Index

JAMES MONTGOMERY BOICE was senior minister of Philadelphia's historic Tenth Presbyterian Church for thirty years, as well as a leading spokesman for the Reformed faith until his death in June 2000. He taught on an international radio broadcast, "The Bible Study Hour," was a prolific author, and served for ten years as chairman of the International Council on Biblical Inerrancy.

CROSSWAY
BOOKS